How to C
Beef, Pork,
Wild Game

Canning, Smoking, Salt Curing, Freezing, Freeze-Drying, Dehydrating & Brining

Great for Camping, Hiking, RV Living & Doomsday Preppers

By

Nick Romano

Published by:

Streets of Dream
Press

Streets of Dream Press

Cover & Interior designed

By

Rebecca Jackson

First Edition

Contents

Special Thanks

This book is dedicated to my Nonno and Nonna, my dear grandparents, who were the biggest influence in my life.

Also, thank you for purchasing and reading this book. I hope you learn something new. As my Nonno has always said, "Never stop learning, because then you'll stop growing."

= = = = = = = =

Would you please consider leaving a review where you purchased this book online? I intend to read the reviews to improve my writing for my next book venture. Thanks in advance!

Introduction

Although our ancestors' ability to create fire might be one of our species' earliest breakthroughs, I would argue and say that our species' survival is also due to the fact that our early ancestors knew how to preserve food. As hunter-gatherers, early humans are nomads - that means they move around and migrate like animals to find food and shelter. It's only later that they started to settle and learned how to cultivate the land. In order to survive the various terrains while roaming around to find the next potential settlement, our early ancestors not only needed warmth but also needed to know how to find food.

According to Maslow's hierarchy of needs, the basic needs are security, safety, warmth, rest, water, and food. In order to survive, a human will need to be able to satisfy the basic needs first above all else - nourish the body first before the mind, as they say. Other things like love, self-esteem, and fulfillment can wait.

Unlike today, food was not always available for our ancestors. It was much harder to survive 300,000 years ago. The lands change; the seasons change. What is there today might not be there tomorrow. So as well as hunting and gathering food, our ancestors needed to find ways on how to preserve the food they have hunted or gathered. Cavemen discovered that by leaving slivers of meat, fruits, and nuts to dry out in the sun, they can prevent them from rotting, and thus food can be stored for longer periods of time.

And so, one of the first signs an archeologist looks for when searching for evidence of an ancient civilization would be broken pots and other vessels. It might not sound like much, but it's an almost certain sign of an ancient settlement or civilization. A scattering of pottery shards across a dig site is history's way of telling us that people lived and ate here, at this place.

Archeologists sometimes find remnants of food in these vessels, thus letting us peek into the lives of our ancestors, that is, what they ate and how they stored them. A steady supply of food is basic for human survival - and in ancient times, the ability to procure and store food was all that stood between certain doom and survival until the next spring.

Born from this need is our journey into finding ways on how to safely store food. Food preservation is a large part of human history. Throughout millennia, before the advent of modern technology, humans from all across the world in different cultures have developed different ways on how they can prolong the shelf life of food, from the various pickled vegetables, brined seafood, and meat jerkies. Preserving food and curing meats is vital knowledge for early humans who are, by nature, hunter-gatherers.

Fast forward to today: we can get food in an instant and without any thought. Supermarkets and groceries are well stocked with everything you can need and want.

Logistics makes it possible for fish caught in Japan to be enjoyed the next day in a trendy sushi bar in LA. People of today never have to think of how to store food to last them throughout winter.

But the practice of food preservation never died. In Korea, kimchi - a type of pickled vegetable - is still consumed daily, as well as copious amounts of preserved vegetables are still enjoyed in different parts of Asia. Curing meats is also elevated into an art form in some cases, like the most expensive ham in the world called Jamon Iberico de bellota from Spain. A leg of this acorn-fed black Iberian pig cured to perfection can cost up to $4,500.

In short, what once was a vital knowledge needed for our survival ages ago is now a delicacy or even an artisanal product in some cases, like the famed hams of Italy and Spain.

But curing meats is not limited to just the dry-cured hams in cellars in Italy. There are numerous ways in how one can preserve food. We can salt, brine, freeze, smoke, and can them. Centuries of human evolution have brought forth a handful of food preservation methods that are still used today.

If you look around the internet, cured meat is in. Humans suddenly have a lot of time in their hands to learn new skill sets during the pandemic. Some have learned how to bake, cook, sew, and some have even taken it upon themselves to step into the world of food preservation. You might think that not a lot of people will have the reasons to cure meat. When I started my channel, I figured I'd just share how my family would cure our meats in our small delicatessen in a crowded part of the world for generations now.

Growing up, I took for granted the slices of delectable hams that Nonno would shove into my mouth when I would watch him slice delicate slivers of meat. To my young eyes, it seemed like he's an artisan when he started the carving process. But it was when I stayed in Italy with my uncle for 4 years that cemented my love for all things charcuterie. I was ready to go back to my Nonno's deli.

We started the channel and the blog as a way to

further our market reach, advertise our new products, and also feature some recipes to go with it. But now, it has grown big enough that we have followers from all over the world leaving comments and asking for more. Nonno loves reading the comments, by the way, and insists on being featured in some of the videos as well.

So to celebrate the milestone for both our deli and our channel, we'll be sharing our knowledge with our dear patrons. This book you have in your hands is a project we have been working on for the last 2 years.

Tracing through our history and after trips to visit our friends over in Italy, we've collected some valuable knowledge that is now in this book you hold in your hands. I've learned so much during this journey, and I hope you will too.

Freezing

The Basics of Freezing

Up in Alaska, when some miners were looking for gold, they found a 50,000-year-old bison instead. This bison named "Blue Babe" was frozen rapidly enough that researchers found that its muscles had frozen while still fresh, with a texture that's not unlike beef jerky. So the researchers figured they'd cut out part of its neck meat, season it, cook it in a stew, and eat it at a dinner party.

As proven by these intrepid researchers, frozen food, if done correctly - or in their case, meets the correct criteria - will last a long time. It is one of the easiest and quickest ways on how you can prolong the shelf life of your food (quickest if you live far up in the icy north - a land where it's eternal day or eternal night depending on the seasons, where ice is everywhere, and where the Inuit people still hunt seals, whales, and polar bears for food).

Hunting in the frozen seas is a hard job, and there will be days when the hunt will not yield anything, so they keep their excess game encased in ice, in a wooden box in the far side of town where it can keep for days and months. In those places, the meat will freeze rapidly enough that it will still retain its freshness after a long while.

But unlike smoking or curing, freezing will not kill off any bacteria that can cause your food to spoil. Freezing will only stop or slow down bacterial growth, so spoilage can still happen if you do not freeze your items in the right way. To keep this from happening, food must be frozen rapidly and be always kept at a temperature of below 0°F.

By keeping your freezer temperature at or below 0°F, you can not only stop the growth of the bacteria that can cause spoilage but also lessen the changes in your foods' texture, nutritive value, and flavor.

Things to Consider

Another thing to think about when you plan to freeze your food is the enzymes that are responsible for them breaking down. These enzymes are responsible for speeding up the ripening process or the maturing process of plants, or even the breaking down of cellular structures in meats. If allowed to continue, these reactions will change the color, flavor, and texture of the food. To stop these, a lot of people will blanch that food quickly or add ascorbic acid to prevent browning.

Blanching means quickly placing the food in boiling water for 30 seconds to a minute and then quickly cooking them in an ice bath. Done mostly with vegetables, this will stop and inactivate the enzymes and also kill any microorganisms on the surface. By blanching your vegetables, you can keep them for longer, and they take less room in your freezer.

To prevent browning on fruits which are usually eaten raw and therefore can't be blanched, chemical compounds like ascorbic acid - also known as Vitamin C - can be used. If you are in a pinch and can't find vitamin C, lemon juice can also be used.

For meats, the most common problem people might have is dealing with rancidity. Freezing meat you are going to cook in a few weeks is fine, especially if you already got it vacuum-packed and frozen. But for fresh meats straight from the butcher that you plan to store for a longer period of time, it is advised to trim off the excess fat and to place them in an airtight wrap or a vacuum-sealed plastic bag.

Taking this extra step will also prevent freezer burn - damage to the meat or any other food stuff caused by moisture loss and exposure to air. While still safe to eat, the meat might develop dark or gray spots, and the surface might appear like leather. Fruits and vegetables, on the other hand, will have their water content turned into ice crystals, making them shrivel and dry out.

One other thing to take into account will be the texture

of the food. Water expands when it freezes, so when you freeze food, the cell walls will break down or rupture when the water inside them freezes. When the food is finally thawed, a lot of them will tend to have a softer or mushy texture. This effect is more apparent in some vegetables and fruits rather than meat due to their higher water content. For this reason, if you ever find frozen chunks of fruits in your freezer, it is best to serve it while it is still partially frozen.

Cooking the food beforehand will soften the cell walls and can lessen these unwanted effects. Food items that are rapidly frozen can produce better results. According to research, the longer it takes for the food to freeze, the larger the ice crystals will be. It will, therefore, also result in larger cell damage. But freezing the food rapidly, on the other hand, will produce smaller ice crystals - which will, in turn, minimize cell damage. This principle is why, most of the time, flash freezing is the method used for freshly caught seafood to ensure its quality for the journey to your table. This is also done to all kinds of meat you usually see sold chilled in the supermarkets, thawed in advance for the shopper's convenience.

Luckily, this method is not only limited to larger manufacturers. You can also do rapid freezing in your home easily - no fancy equipment is required. All you need is a freezer, and luckily, that freezer in your fridge will do well most of the time.

Choosing the Right Container

Pack meats using proper containers. Different food items require slightly different containers too. Be careful not to use containers that are too large as they will cause the items to freeze slowly, which is counterintuitive to our goal. As a guide, containers you can use for the freezer should be:

Food grade

Moisturize proof

Waterproof

Durable

Odorless

Leakproof

Designed for the freezer, meaning it shouldn't crack or be brittle after prolonged use in the freezer.

There are different types of materials that are used to make freezer-grade containers: plastic resealable freezer bags, rigid and resealable metal, glass or plastic containers, and flexible or soft plastic/silicone containers. Carefully read the back labels of any containers you plan to buy. They should be clearly marked as good for freezer use. Most manufacturers would also include temperature limits for their products. Choose items that can withstand temperatures lower than 0°F.

Rigid containers are great for keeping liquid, soft, or food that can easily be broken down. The straight and hard sides make it easy for the food to be removed with just the application of a wet towel on the outside surface of the container. Most of them are also designed to nest or stack on top of each other. These containers are mostly made of metal and plastic materials. Glass can also be used, but again it should be specified that it is tested good for freezer use as normal glass containers like jars for canning can easily crack when temperatures reach below freezing. When you do use rigid containers, make sure the lids close tightly, so it's airtight. If they are not, it is recommended to use freezer tapes - tapes designed for temperatures below freezing. Do not use masking tapes as they may not stick properly.

The most commonly used are the resealable plastic freezer bags and wraps that are widely available in stores. In a pinch, heavy-duty aluminum foil can also be used. Keep them away from sharp objects and corners inside the freezer to prevent puncturing - the use of cardboard dividers in the freezer can protect the plastic wraps and aluminum foils. These bags are perfect for drier food items like chops and steaks or pieces of raw meat, fish, and poultry; fruits and vegetables are suitable for these.

Another type of container that has recently gained traction in social media is the resealable silicone container that can also double as a freezer container. Since it's a mix between the rigid and the softer and more flexible wraps and bags, a lot of people are now opting for it as it's more durable than the plastic freezer bags. Plus, it's a more environmentally safer alternative than freezer bags.

Procedure for Freezing Meats at Home

If you plan on freezing fresh meats at home, it is recommended to turn on the freezer and keep the temperature inside well below freezing - around -10°F or even lower - for a few hours in advance.

The meat you are planning to use within a week or so can just be placed in the freezer in their original packaging, but for items, you plan to store for longer periods of time, you need to properly package your meat and seal it. When packing for the long term, keep your meats away from air and try to store them in an airtight or vacuum-sealed freezer bag to keep them from freezer burn. For fresh meats you just brought home from stores, you must try to work quickly and efficiently so the meat won't have enough time to completely thaw when you're working. Remember to keep your countertop, hands, utensils, and equipment clean to prevent contamination. You must pay particular attention to cleanliness when handling raw poultry to avoid food poisoning. Also, remember to clean and disinfect after to keep your family safe.

To maintain the quality of the meat, the freezer temperature must be maintained below 0°F even when it's finished with the initial freeze. If food is allowed to be stored in a freezer with a temperature above 0°F, it might result in spoilage and possibly a shorter shelf life. Frozen food should be kept frozen.

Place it in the coldest parts of the freezer - on most freezers, these are against the walls. Take care not to overload the space. Cramming your freezer with unfrozen food all at the same time will lead to a slow freeze.

Red Meat

If you are a hunter or a butcher, freezing your red meats might be the easiest and fastest thing you could do to them when you have a lot, and you still haven't found the time or the right recipe to make your summer sausage.

When you go to a butcher or a deli, most will gladly do a quick freeze for you. It's perfect for when you don't want to cook your meat just yet. You can just store them in the freezer when you get home.

To freeze red meat is relatively simple. You just need to keep them away from moisture and air to keep the quality. Cut and trim the excess fat and take out all the bones if you can. If you purchase fresh meat from the store or your butcher, it may come wrapped in a simple butcher paper. Meats wrapped in the store with butcher papers or any other paper wraps cannot be counted upon to keep your meats from getting freezer burned.

It is always better to take them out and rewrap them in a freezer bag or in a freezer-safe container if you don't plan on using them within the week you bought them. If you don't plan on removing the butcher paper, just over-wrapping them with a freezer-grade wrap or placing them in a freezer-proof bag will do. However, for items that are bought vacuum sealed and frozen, there would be a need to rewrap them. Just refreezing them after you get home is fine.

Additionally, if you are to store or pack several individual cuts of meat in one package or container, you should place freezer paper or baking paper in between each piece to prevent them from freezing together for easier thawing. You can also choose to tray pack smaller chunks of meat or cut pieces of poultry. To tray pack means freezing your meats in a baking tray, arranged, so the items do not touch each other. Cover the tray with a freezer-safe plastic wrap and freeze until everything is completely frozen. You can then transfer these into smaller, more compact containers for easier storage.

Salted meats like hams and luncheon meats, even though already cured, are not suited to be stored in the freezer. You will find that the salt inside the cured meats will make your meats become rancid faster. For other cured meats, like hotdogs and luncheon meats, the freezing temperatures will make the emulsions inside break down and will cause it to leak, leaving the meat to "weep."

For cooked meats, the lower temperatures will make the meat dry out much faster than raw meat. So it is highly recommended to actually store it with the sauce you cooked it in. Submerge or coat your meats with gravy and seal in a bag or a container. You will find that after thawing your meats, they will have retained their freshness as well as becoming more flavorful for having had more time to absorb the sauce. But keep in mind that meats frozen in sauces or marinades will last a lot shorter when compared to fresh raw meat. Try to consume them within 3 months.

Poultry

When choosing poultry that is best for freezing, it is better to choose whole, fresh, and unblemished ones. Select plump and odorless ones to ensure freshness. You can definitely choose to purchase poultry that has already been butchered, but it is definitely worth it to take time to learn how to properly cut up your poultry. It is a lot easier than it looks and absolutely a lot easier than butchering beef or pork.

To butcher poultry, pull and separate the legs and wings from the body, then separate the thigh from the drumstick. Chop the ribcage separating the back from the breast, splitting it in half. If you want, you can further chop the breast in half for smaller servings.

When choosing the correct poultry to freeze, keep in mind how you intend to cook it. If you are planning to cook stews, choose more flavorful birds. Young birds, on the other hand, are perfect for roasting and frying.

Before you freeze your poultry, prepare it according to how you are planning to use it in the future. Birds you plan to cut up for intended recipes need to be chopped up before you freeze them. The same goes for birds you plan to cook half or whole. But for stuffed poultry, do not freeze the stuffing inside the bird. The stuffing has a higher probability of harboring poisonous bacteria during thawing and refreezing. You can freeze the stuffing but keep it separated from the poultry. The same goes for the giblets or the gizzard, heart, liver, and neck; pack them separately as they go bad faster, around 2 weeks. These are great when used to make gravy or add to your stuffing.

When packing chopped-up birds, do the same as you would with other red meats. Place freezer papers in between individual portions for easier separation when you take them out. You can also tray pack individual pieces of poultry.

Like the red meats, fresh poultry you buy in butcher shops and stores will normally come wrapped with butcher papers. These papers are not enough to protect your birds from getting burned in the freezer. If you are planning to store these birds in your freezer for longer than a week, rewrap or overwrap them again unless they come to you vacuum-sealed. If they are, do not open them and just store them straight inside the freezer.

Fish

Fish is much harder to prepare than red meat as they go bad quite easily. If you catch them fresh, other than gutting, descaling, and cleaning them, you need to salt them or dunk them in an ascorbic acid solution to make them keep better in the fridge. So if you are buying them from your fishmonger, ask them to do the gutting, cleaning, and descaling for you. This will make your freezing preparation go much faster when you get home.

Freshly caught fish needs to be frozen right away, so if you are out in a lake and you are not planning to go home just yet, keep your fish packed deep within in a large cooler filled with crushed ice. When you get home, wash the fish thoroughly in fresh potable water, then descale the fish by running the back of your knife repeatedly back and forth against the skin gently. Make a cut on the belly of the fish to get all the entrails out. Be careful not to puncture the innards when you make the cut - this will lend a bitter taste to your fish. Chop the head of the fish off and then rinse everything in fresh potable water again, paying close attention to the stomach cavity of the fish.

Next, using a sharp knife, remove the back fins as well as the dorsal fins. Cut from the base and take care not to leave stumps of the fins in the fish. It is better to cut along the side of the fish to cleanly remove all the fins. Rinse the fish again in water. For larger fishes, it is recommended to chop them up or be filleted for easier cooking after taking them out of the freezer. For larger fish like tuna or salmon and large Spanish mackerels, cut them in ¾ inch thick steaks crosswise.

To fillet medium-sized fish, make a cut all along the back of the fish from the collarbone to the tail. Make another cut along the tail of the fish, positioning your knife flat and slice the flesh off, running the knife along the spine, from the tail to the collarbone. Flip the flesh off and do the same procedure on the other side of the fish. Run the back of your knife along the spine of the fish to feel for fish bones still stuck inside the flesh. Use a tweezer to pull all the fish bones out.

Pre-treat the fish before freezing to improve the quality. This will decrease the rancidity as well as the probability of flavor change. For fish that have higher fat content like tuna, salmon, mackerel, trout, and mullet, dip them in an ascorbic acid solution for around 20 to 30 seconds. To make the solution, mix 2 teaspoons of ascorbic acid (crystalline) and 1 quart of fresh potable water. For lean fish like snapper, grouper, flounder, cod, croaker, redfish, whiting, and most freshwater ones like bass, catfish, and crappie, it is enough to sink them in a brine for 20 to 30 seconds. To make the brine solution, mix ¼ cup of salt with 1 quart of fresh and cold potable water. This solution will make the flesh firm up and also decrease the drip loss when you thaw the fish.

After the pretreatment, you can freeze fish in 3 different ways. The easiest is to wrap in a freezer wrap or place it in a freezer bag. Remove air from the bag and place straight into the freezer. Remember to place freezer paper or baking paper in between individual slices before freezing as you would do with individual pieces of meat and poultry for easier thawing.

You can also choose to place it in a rigid container and cover it with fresh potable water, then freeze it. Make sure all parts of the fish are covered with water and cover the container tightly with an airtight lid or with a freezer-safe wrap.

Alternatively, you can do the ice glaze method. This method is mostly done with those vacuum-packed, frozen fish that are typically sold in supermarkets. To do this, place the fish - whole, cut or filleted - unwrapped and separate in a tray and freeze. Once it is completely frozen, dunk the fish or the individual pieces of it separately quickly into very cold, fresh potable water, then place it back in the freezer. Do this, dunking and refreezing for a couple of times until a uniform and visible film of hard ice is coating the fish. This will create a thin protective layer of water on the surface of the fish, protecting it from the harsh environment of the freezer. After, place the ice glazed fish in a freezer bag and store it in the freezer. Also, remember to keep individual pieces separate from each other.

For fish roe - which is a delicacy in its own right - it should be frozen separately. Roe can be considered the most perishable part of the fish and should be carefully taken out of the stomach cavity and washed thoroughly with fresh potable water. To prepare the egg sacs for freezing, pierce the sacs with a clean and disinfected needle in different locations, then dunk it in an ascorbic acid solution like you would do with fatty fish. A 20 second to 30-second dip would be sufficient. This will also decrease the effect of rancidity and change of flavor on the fish eggs when you store them in the freezer. Afterward, wrap the egg sacs in individual freezer wraps or bags and freeze. Remember to use the roe all up within 3 months or so.

Game

For hunters who want to store their fresh-caught wild game in the freezer, field dress and process large animals like deer, antelope, and moose to prevent it from spoiling. Butcher it and clean the meat, then freeze it as you would do with the other red meats. Cut and throw away the bloodshot meat before you freeze the meat. This will go bad faster and should be thrown away.

For small game like squirrels and rabbits, these should be skinned, dressed, and refrigerated or chilled as soon as possible after killing them. Keep it refrigerated for a day or 2 until you find that the meat is pliable and no longer rigid. Prepare them or cut the meat according to how you intend to cook them in the future. Pack and freeze like you would do with the other red meats.

Game birds - duck, geese, dove, quail, and pheasant - these birds should be bled, plucked of feathers, gutted, cleaned, and refrigerated or chilled right after shooting. Remember to trim or cut off any excess fat to prevent rancidity, especially for geese and ducks. Pack and freeze these game birds the same as you would with the other poultry.

Thawing

It is highly recommended to thaw meat, fish, and poultry in the fridge to prevent the growth of bacteria that can cause spoilage. For meats like steaks and other large cuts of meat or whole poultry you are planning to roast or use in stews, these should be partially thawed before you can place them in a pot or in an oven to cook. Partially thawing larger chunks of meat and poultry will prevent them from being overdone on the outside and undercooked or even raw in the center.

On the other hand, for frozen meats, fish, and poultry you plan to coat with breading or batter before cooking, they should also be partially thawed so the breading batter will have a higher chance of sticking to the surface. It is better to completely thaw frozen food when you plan to cook them by deep-frying. The high heat and quick cooking time will quickly cook the outside while the inside or center will stay frozen.

Cooking frozen meat will generally take a long time and should be done slowly over a low fire. Cooking in high heat will result in unbalanced cooking - you'll find that the surface will char or cook quickly, but the inside will remain cold and frozen. If this can happen easily for chilled or refrigerated items, then the probability of serving a charred but frozen inside roast will be higher with frozen meats. Depending on the size of the cuts, frozen food will generally take half or twice as long as you normally would with chilled or room temperature meat, fish, or poultry.

Generally, there are 3 different methods on how you can go about thawing your meats, poultry, and fish straight from the freezer. The slowest and safest would be to thaw the sealed packages in the fridge. Place it on top of a tray or place to catch the drippings and prevent meltwater from flooding your fridge. The smaller cuts will, of course, thaw much more quickly, taking only a few hours, but larger whole birds and bigger cuts of meat may take you a whole day or so until you'll find them completely defrosted.

An old method to thaw or defrost frozen food is to submerge the sealed package in a bowl filled with room temperature water. Keep changing the water every half an hour until the item is completely unfrozen. With this method, the items must be cooked immediately after they are thawed to prevent spoilage.

When you purchase microwaves, a lot of them will have the defrost option included. These can also be used to defrost your meats, fish, and poultry as long as they fit nicely inside the oven. You might need to turn and flip the items while defrosting so everything is thawed evenly. As with the old method of submerging it with water, food items thawed in the microwave must also be cooked immediately after they are defrosted.

Frozen meats, fish, and poultry must never be left on the countertop to defrost at room temperature. This will make the bacteria multiply quickly, spoiling your food.

Defrosted raw food items must be defrosted completely and cooked before you can safely freeze them again. Thawing or defrosting and freezing again will make the ice crystals become larger than you would normally want. This will rupture the cell walls of the meat, causing the quality of the meat to degrade over time. So it is better to cook them after defrosting before freezing them again to minimize the loss of moisture, flavor, and quality. However, if you defrost an item inside the refrigerator and you suddenly find yourself changing your mind and need to freeze them again, it is totally safe to do so. But doing so will definitely affect the quality of the meat.

Storage Shelf Life: Storage Times for Food

Although food stored in a freezer can keep for long periods of time, the quality and nutrition degrade over time. Don't try to store it for 50,000 years - even though food stored in the freezer can last you indefinitely. It is still a little bit dodgy to eat beef that has been in the back of your freezer for over a decade. Here's a handy table for how long you can store food in your freezer.

Seafood

Fatty fish (perch, salmon, and mackerel): 2 to 3 months

Lean fish (flounder, cod, and sole): 3 to 6 months

Cooked fish: 4 to 6 months

Smoked fish (sealed and vacuum-packed): 2 months

Shellfish (mussels, oysters, scallops, etc.): 3 to 6 months

Shrimp: 3 to 5 months

Cooked crab: 2 months

Processed Meat

Bacon: 1 to 2 months

Luncheon meat (opened/sealed package or sliced in the deli): 1 to 2 months

Burgers and ground meat patties (made from beef, pork, poultry, veal, lamb, etc.): 3 to 4 months

Hot dogs (opened or sealed): 1 to 2 months

Sausages (made from beef, chicken, pork, or turkey)

Raw: 1 to 2 months

Cooked: 1 to 2 months

Pre-frozen: 2 months

Ham

Fresh; uncooked and uncured: 5 to 6 month

Fresh; cooked and uncured: 3 to 4 month

Cured, cooked, and vacuum sealed (unopened): 1 to 2 months

Comes country ham: 1 month

Canned and unopened (labeled with "keep refrigerated"): no need to freeze; will keep in the fridge for 6 to 9 months

Canned and opened (shelf-stable): 1 to 2 months

Italian and Spanish hams (Parma, Prosciutto, Serrano, etc.): 1 month

Fresh Ground Meat

lamb and beef: 2 to 3 months

pork: 1 to 2 months

Fresh Whole Slices of Meat (For Steaks and Chops)

Beef: 6 to 12 months

Pork: 3 to 6 months

Veal and lamb: 1 to 2 months

Fresh Meat (For Roasts)

Beef: 6 to 12 months

Pork: 3 to 6 months

Lamb and veal: 6 to 9 months

Poultry

Whole chicken: 12 months

Chopped or cut chicken: 6 months

Whole turkey: 12 months

Chopped or cut turkey: 6 months

Whole goose and duck: 6 months

Giblets: 3 months

Wild game (uncooked): 8 to 12 months

Cooked and Pre-cooked Food

Stews or casseroles (meat, poultry, and fish): 3 months

Meat pies: 3 months

Fruit pies (unbaked): 8 months

Fruit pies (baked): 2 to 4 months

Bread: 3 months

Cake: 3 months

Cookies (baked and unbaked): 3 months

Dairy

Butter: 6 to 9 months

Margarine: 12 months

Fresh milk: 1 month

Heavy cream: 2 months

Whipped cream: 1 month

Ice cream: 2 months

Organic and natural cheeses: 5 to 8 weeks

Processed cheeses: 4 months

Eggs

(Raw eggs keep better in the freezer when beaten)

Raw beaten eggs: 12 months

Raw eggs (in shells): 12 months; but keep refrigerated to thaw

Overall, food stored properly in below freezing temperatures will last you for a long time, even indefinitely, but for safety's sake, be cautious if the frozen item has been sleeping at the back of a freezer for years. As a general rule, don't consume food that looks and smells off or bad to prevent food poisoning.

Considerations When Freezing Food

Arrange items inside your freezer so that there is space between each one to allow enough cold air to circulate, allowing for an equal freeze. Only stack items on top of each other when everything is fully frozen.

Refrain from opening and closing your freezer multiple times a day. The constant fluctuation of temperature will cause repeated thawing and freezing of the items inside the freezer. Even incremental fluctuations within the freezer will cause the smaller ice crystals to become bigger over time, which will lead to further damage within the cell structure of the meat, leading to a softer and mushier texture in the long run. Temperature fluctuations will also cause water to seep out of the meat, making it less juicy and less healthy.

If freezing cooked meat, freeze them with the sauce, gravy, or the marinade mixed in the bag. This can also prevent moisture loss as well as freezer burn.

For pre-cooked food, let it cool down to room temperature first before storing it in the freezer. Food items that are still hot require a lot more energy to cool down and freeze, raising your electricity bill. Letting your items cool down to room temperature not only slows up the freezing process but can also help maintain their quality more.

Some loose food items like fruits, vegetables, and smaller prices of meat can be tray-packed. Tray-packed items are first arranged in a tray to be quickly frozen in a way that individual pieces are not touching one another or in one thin layer that can be easily broken up when frozen. The items are then gathered and placed in a smaller container or bag for easier access. Examples of items that can be tray-packed are berries, broccoli, chopped chicken, chicken wings, patties, and nuggets.

If you do not have a vacuum sealer, you don't need to buy one if you are just freezing a small number of items for your home. Note that this is not vacuum packing as you will not be able to remove all the air inside the bag. But to do this, fill a large bowl with water and place your meat inside a resealable freezer bag. Zip it nearly close until you have around a quarter of an inch left open. Slowly submerge the bag in the water, pulling down slowly until all the air is pushed out and only the tip left open is above the water. Seal it close.

Butter and margarine, when cut and separated by smaller pieces of parchment or baking paper, can also be kept in the freezer. Cut the butter or margarine while still cool into smaller flat squares. Insert pieces of parchment paper in between and freeze.

Try to portion out the items by the number of servings you plan to use. This will prevent the repeated thawing that can ruin the quality of your food.

Water will expand when frozen, so your food will also expand when frozen. Try to give your meats a little wiggle room when you are packing them in resealable plastic bags to prevent leakage.

Label your items properly before staking them in the fridge. This will save you a lot of time searching for the right items. It also minimizes the time the freezer is kept open while you're searching.

Defrost or thaw food inside the fridge; place a tray or a plate under to catch the juices. Do not leave food to thaw in a warm place as it might spoil.

Freeze Drying

What is Freeze Drying?

Along with freezing, there is another ancient method called freeze-drying that you can use to preserve your food. Freeze drying, unlike how the name implies, is different from the above methods I just discussed. Freeze drying is technically another form of dehydration.

The Incan empire once spread all over the unforgiving land of the Andes. They thrived in that harsh, unforgiving landscape that was absolutely freezing at night but at the same time was windy and dry. They made chuño - a form of freeze-dried potatoes that could last for years and sustained their massive armies for years. It was made by Altiplano villagers who live in the high plateaus of Peru and Bolivia. There's black and white chuño, the former being made by leaving the harvested bitter potatoes outside to freeze overnight and crushing them with their feet in the day to remove the skin and squeeze out the liquids until it's completely dehydrated or the latter by soaking or submerging the potatoes in the freezing waters of the local streams and rivers then leaving them out to dry out in the sun after.

It is still eaten today in the Andes. Locals love it, but the taste makes it hard for foreigners to get used to. It is eaten as you would with freezer-dried mashed potatoes by just adding water. The locals add it to other local dishes where a potato can be used, like the local chili or aji, or ground to powder form to make them into flour that can be used to make slurries to thicken stews and soups. The long shelf life can also save the livelihood of these local people who rely on a good harvest in order to live. If the crops go bad this year, at least they have stored chuño to help them get by.

So why does this method make the food last so long? It is said that the chalk-like dehydrated potatoes of the Andes can rival the shelf life of modern freeze-dried food. In dehydration, you draw out the moisture from the food with heat. Dehydration will draw out around 95% of the water content inside the food, while food that had its moisture drawn out by freeze-drying will have around 99% of water content drawn out from the food. This method thus will give your food longer shelf life and will generally taste better than its dehydrated counterparts. Even though "freeze" is part of the name, you don't need to store freeze-dried foods inside the freezer or even in the fridge. Freeze-dried foods, once packaged properly in airtight and vacuum-sealed mylar bags, can last you for a long time, even if you just store them in your cupboard.

Also, due to the method on how the water content is drawn out from the food items, freeze-dried food will also rehydrate easily and quickly, making it the perfect way to process food that you plan to store for a very long time. Rehydrated freeze-dried food can also be used as you would normally with fresh food. For example, if you freeze-dried pieces of raw bacon, you can rehydrate it with just a bowl of fresh potable water, and it's ready to be cooked like you would with normal freshly bought bacon. Cooked food, like stews, roasts, soups, and stir-fried foods, can also be freeze-dried with little loss to flavor and quality. And when opened, freeze-dried food is generally recommended to be consumed within 4 months.

It is for this reason that NASA favors this method when packing food for our astronauts to take to space. It is brought into space in compact little bags that astronauts can easily rehydrate quickly with just a little water. Preppers also favor this method to preserve meats and other cooked food for their bunkers and go bags as they will last you indefinitely. The downside is you will need water to rehydrate raw food items in order to safely consume them, but meals cooked before freeze-drying will generally be safe to consume when opened and rehydrated. But due to its dehydrated nature, it will absorb water from other sources, like your saliva or from inside your stomach, so you will be rehydrating the food one way or another.

For natural disasters that only last a few days without access to freshwater, freeze-dried food will be very useful or even life-saving. But for disasters that will make you stay out without any access to clean water for days or weeks, consumption of freeze-dried food should be limited, and water should be saved for drinking. Freeze-dried food should also be avoided by backpackers or climbers. Activities that make you sweat a lot and expend energy will dehydrate your body. Eating freeze-dried food on top of it all will not only add to your body's dehydration but also "back up" your gastrointestinal tract as it will absorb more water from your body as it goes on its way out. So if you do bring with you freeze-dried food when you are out climbing or camping, be sure to pack with you lots of water and electrolyte-filled drinks that can help you rehydrate properly.

When food is freeze-dried, the food will undergo a process called lyophilization. Food will be brought down to temperatures that are below freezing. Then the water content is removed when vacuum pressure is applied to the food. It is extracted in vapor form, which then condenses back into ice in the machine's condenser. The temperature is then gradually brought back up to allow for the remaining moisture to be extracted from the food while retaining the structure of the food, which is useful for when you want to rehydrate the food again in the future.

Almost any food item can be freeze-dried, though some will fare better than others. The meat you plan to freeze-dry will need to be cut up into smaller chunks to be more suitable for this method as smaller-sized food will fare better when undergoing this method. Coffee, soups, and other liquids do well after freeze-drying too. In fact, most of the instant coffees we regularly ingest to keep us alert and alive are either made by freeze-drying or by spray drying. Freeze-dried fruits and vegetables are also gaining traction in the stores, being sold and marketed as being healthier alternatives to dehydrated foods.

However, you will find that a freeze-drying machine is very expensive. It will definitely set you back by around $2000 to $4000 for one machine. But on the bright side, you really don't need to shell out that much money if you are only freeze-drying a small amount of food yearly.

Although the methods listed under are categorized as freeze-drying methods, especially by a few enterprising internet bloggers, they will not yield a freeze-dried product. In fact, they do not really freeze dry food. They are more like just storing your food in the freezer like the above methods I've discussed above. You will really need a machine or a vacuum to remove all the moisture from your food items for it to be called freeze-dried food. It is also not very time efficient. For a freeze-drying machine to finish one load, it will generally take you around 20 to 40 hours or even longer.

At this point, you will really be going back into the freezer method. Sure the early Incans discovered the basics of how they can freeze dry food up in the high and really dry altitudes. But unless you can recreate their climate, then freeze-drying food in your home will definitely be a struggle and will be better if you can just buy freeze-dried food from your local grocer. I've tried this method again and again just for research when writing this book, but it does not freeze dry anything. It just freezes the food and exposes it to freezer burn. I strongly advise you to stick to normal freezing if you do not have a machine.

If you want to experiment and satisfy your curiosity since this method is prevalent on the internet, the freezer you'll be using must be able to reach temperatures that are far below freezing. Your food at this stage will risk getting freezer burned as you'll be exposing it to below negative temperatures as well as letting it stay there uncovered for around 4 weeks to give it time to be dehydrated. It is said that to check if your food has been totally dehydrated, you can test it out by bringing it out of the freezer and letting it thaw to room temperature slowly. If it turns black, then you have not been successful, and it's back to the drawing board again. If it retains its color and physical structure, then you have successfully frozen and semi-dried your food. Doing this method will turn your food into mush when thawed. You have been warned.

If you really do this, you will need to have a very large freezer that is also relatively odorless to keep your food items that are in the process of freeze-drying from acquiring other unwanted smells from the freezer.

Another way that has been suggested is to use dry ice. For this process, be sure to use protective equipment as dry ice can actually burn your skin. To freeze using the dry ice method, place the food items inside a freezer bag. Leave it open as the escaping air might make your bag explode. On top of the freezer bag, pile a large amount of dry ice and leave it to dry out for 24 hours. After 24 hours, the container or freezer will be filled with carbon dioxide, so do this in a well-ventilated room. Inhaling carbon dioxide in enclosed spaces can definitely cause death. If successful, food that's been frozen using dry ice will need to be stored in vacuum-sealed airtight containers, and be careful not to let any moisture enter the bag.

Another method that will surely come up when you search the net if you want to freeze dry items at home is liquid nitrogen. Liquid nitrogen, of course, will freeze food very quickly as soon as it comes into contact with it. At -320°F, liquid nitrogen will freeze anything that it comes in contact with and should be handled carefully. A lot of the time, liquid nitrogen will come in as the faster way to bring the food to below freezing temperature before a vacuum pump can extract all the moisture from the food. If you do not have a drying machine, you can still use liquid nitrogen to flash freeze your food before you can store it in the freezer.

Rapid freezing will maintain the quality of your food the best when compared to normal freezing in the freezer, as it produces smaller ice crystals. Since liquid nitrogen will flash freeze the items, little damage to the quality of the meats, poultry, and fish will happen therefore retaining its quality quite effectively. And unlike normal freezing, the very low temperature will also be able to kill any bacteria or pathogen that can make your food go bad.

Or you can go really old school and do it the Inca way - flash freeze it, and leave it outside to dry out in the sun and hope for the best.

To end this, when compared to dehydrating, the latter will be much more cost-effective for home use. Freeze drying cannot be made in your home unless you buy thousands of dollars of equipment. Unless you have a farm or are planning a freeze-drying business, it is best to stick with normal freezing and dehydration.

Freeze Drying with a Freeze Dryer Machine

If you're planning a large-scale freeze-drying empire or

you just really want to try out freeze-drying, then it might be time for you to actually purchase one of these machines. If you have a farm or even a fruit farm, acquiring a freeze-drying machine will definitely be a worthy investment. Note that having a freeze dryer in your home will not save you a lot of time if you want to prep food for storage quickly. If you want quick and efficient, other methods will be better for you. You cannot overload the trays and containers. And the drying time will take a 1-day minimum for thin slices of meat and fruits to around 3 days for thicker and larger chunks of food.

But to get into the deep end of freeze-drying, you need to know that there are actually 3 steps that need to happen for a satisfying freeze-dried product to come out. And you can either just buy a freeze-drying machine, or if you are feeling adventurous, you can rig something together by watching YouTube tutorials. There are a lot out there that can teach you how to wrangle up a vacuum chamber in your home.

So, for a DIY home freeze drying rig, the first is the freezing part. You will need a heavy-duty freezer that can have the temperatures drop to -30°F or even colder. Alternatively, as stated above, you can flash freeze the items with liquid nitrogen for this stage. Second, you will need a completely airtight vacuum-sealed chamber and a vacuum pump to draw the moisture out of your food items. This second part is called the primary drying or sublimation process.

Lastly comes the desorption or the secondary drying process. You must attach a thermostat and a heater to the rig so you can add heat in the chamber slowly to draw the rest of the moisture out. This step is needed so you can bump the temperature inside the chamber up and down to repeat the sublimation process again and again. A humidity sensor is also needed - this will let you know if all the moisture is taken out of your food items.

Armed with this knowledge, you now need to ask yourself a few questions before embarking on your freeze-drying journey. What are you going to use it for? Will it just be for camping or backpacking purposes? Do you bulk buy a lot of stuff and plan to freeze-dry cooked items for your family meals? Or are you a doomsday prepper prepping for the apocalypse or nuclear fallout? Whatever your reason is, buying even a home freeze drying machine is going to be a huge investment.

It is better to actually think through your reasons. You don't want a piece of thousand-dollar equipment you'll only use just once to be gathering dust in your basement or garage. Besides, these machines are huge and heavy and will take a large chunk of your kitchen space.

Vacuum Packing

Vacuum Packing Basics

Food will spoil and deteriorate a lot faster when it is exposed to air and room temperature. Early in human history, people discovered this and thus came out with ways on how they can isolate food from the air. Thus canning, bottling, and potting as ways to preserve food became popular. Vacuum packing, also called ROP (reduced oxygen packing), is a relatively new technology that can replace canning and is now an increasingly more popular way to pack and preserved meat, fish, and poultry products.

Vacuum sealing preserves food by cutting off most of its contact with oxygen by using a power pump to suck out all the air in specialized packaging. This prevents the bacteria and pathogens that can cause food spoilage from growing and multiplying. It then uses heat to create an airtight seal around the package. Basically, like most living things, most bacteria and pathogens need oxygen to survive. By cutting off their supply of oxygen, you are effectively killing them, thus preventing your food from going bad.

At the same time, the specialized plastic used in vacuum packing also has the ability to form a barricade against other unwanted elements from the environment from affecting the taste, texture, and smell of the food. It also prevents moisture loss from the food by sealing in the food's moisture content.

And by effectively protecting the food from all these external factors, vacuum packing meats, poultry, and fish can extend the sell-by date and the shelf life of fresh produce by around 3 to 5 times when compared to just the freezing method. Because of this, this relatively new method of preservation is now widely used to package poultry (whole or individual pieces), smoked fish, or slivers of meat.

However, just vacuum packing itself will not be enough to protect your produce from spoilage. Cutting off or reducing the food's contact with oxygen will not kill all the bacteria and pathogens that reside in your produce. Bacteria are a hardy bunch, and unfortunately, some of them can actually live off in a very low oxygen environment. There are even some bacteria - listeria and botulism - that can live and thrive in food that have been vacuum-sealed, but you won't notice a thing since they won't be making any visible changes in the foods' appearance or even smell.

Additionally, even though vacuum-sealed food items will last longer than other food preserved using other methods, vacuum packing, in the end, will only remove or lower the probability of your food coming in contact with oxygen, while other factors will still continue to affect the meat. So, it is recommended that you also watch out for the temperature, moisture content, pH levels, time, and also the amount of oxygen you actually managed to remove from the items.

Other food preservation methods should also be used alongside it when you are vacuum-sealing food items. This is especially true if you are planning to keep the food items for longer periods of time. Vacuum sealed food works the best when done for meats, fish, and poultry you plan to store in the freezer. The seal will effectively protect it from freezer burn and will help the food items retain freshness even when you just keep it chilling in the fridge.

If fresh red meat is wrapped and stored in a freezer correctly, it will probably last around 6 months. When it is vacuum-sealed and stored in the freezer, it can last you up to 2 to 3 years. Surprisingly, vacuum-packed cooked beef will have a shorter lifespan - around 3 months - and around 4 months for cooked poultry.

Generally, the most common material you see used for vacuum packing is plastic - we use this too in our deli to pack our meats and hams. These plastic bags are manufactured specifically for vacuum sealing. Other plastics and bags like those normal freezer bags cannot be used as a substitute. Metal cans are mostly used in commercial production. These are stainless steel cans that have a lid with silicone seals that will create an airtight as well as a watertight seal when closed. There are also glass versions of these metal cans; they are also watertight and airtight. They also come with silicone seals for vacuum sealing.

But vacuum sealing is not only limited to commercial use. You can easily buy home-use vacuum sealers. There are two kinds out in the market: the external and the internal sealers. By concept, both will be extracting all the air out and as well as using heat to seal the bag.

External sealers or non-chamber vacuum sealers only seal one end of the bag. The opening will be fed into the machine, and a retractable nozzle will suck all the air out while the bag is sealed with heat. Unfortunately, because of the retractable hose, you cannot vacuum pack items with liquids. You can find these sealers a lot less expensive and smaller than the internal sealers and are thus perfect for home use.

Internal sealers or single vacuum chamber machines, on the other hand, are also called chamber-type sealers. With this machine, the whole plastic bag is placed inside the machine, which then seals the bag precisely and thoroughly. When the bag is placed in the chamber, the air is sucked out of it and heat is applied all around to seal all sides. At the same time, air is added into the chamber to pressurize it.

The added air pressure will be responsible for pushing out any remaining air in the bag. These machines are bigger and more expensive and thus are usually used and seen in a more commercial environment. This is perfect for people who plan to use it very frequently and plan to seal up items in high volumes.

Considerations Before Purchasing a Machine

Before you purchase your own vacuum packing machine, here are some things you should consider or know about before going ahead with your purchase. There will be different types of vacuum packing machines out there, so get something that fits your lifestyle.

Get something that makes cleaning a breeze. Preparing produce and cleaning up is already a time-consuming job, so you want a machine that makes life easier for you. You'll find that some machines are actually dishwasher-friendly. You can consider getting those for ease of cleaning.

If you are going to be processing items that will have a lot of liquids or sauces with them, consider getting a machine that also comes with an anti-drip tray to catch the accidental spills. The spilled liquid will get sucked into the machine during the vacuum process and can ruin your machine. So be very careful when handling items with high liquid content.

Machines that can seal mason jars and other metal and glass containers are much more expensive, but if you want to invest in something that is more environmentally responsible, then these machines will be worth considering. With these kinds of machines, you will be able to seal a large variety of items from jars to bags, so it might be worth every penny in the long run.

Some machines can accept a large range of bags that you can use for sealing, while some will only accept a certain type of bag for use. So be careful and ask about the types of bags you can use with the machine. Specifically, ask for machines that accept those bags that come in rolls and your normal Ziploc bags as they are significantly cheaper.

There will be some machines that have the added feature of being able to pump inert gasses into your bags. These are useful for when you want to seal in dried food items like coffee beans, nuts, and others. Otherwise, it will not be that useful for you.

When you are scouting for a potential machine, you will stumble upon machines that have double bar heating, which can double seal your bags. Although single sealers are very much adequate for home use, double sealers will be great if you want to double the strength of the seal.

On that note, the sealing bars also vary in size across machines. The commercial machines have sealing bars that measure up to 40 cm, and the ones for home use can go as low as 12.5 cm. Larger sealers are, of course, perfect for when you want to pack large quantities of produce, so it will be nice to be sure about what kind of items you will be using the vacuum sealers for. It is also better to buy something that is a bit bigger than what you think you'll be intending to use it for.

Considerations For Vacuum Sealing

As you would with other food preservation methods, there are a few things that you must keep in mind when you are vacuum sealing.

Work in a clean environment. Keep all surfaces, countertops, equipment, and utensils clean and disinfected to prevent contamination. This also extends to your hands. Personal hygiene should be maintained, and always remember to wash your hands thoroughly before it comes in contact with anything.

If packing raw produce, always choose the freshest ones. Avoid chilled meat, poultry, and fish from the supermarkets. Most of these are flash-frozen for delivery and thawed in store.

Even with your hands scrubbed clean, make a habit of using utensils or gloves when you are handling food, especially raw meat, fish, and poultry.

Don't cross-contaminate - always wash and disinfect everything after processing one product. Be particularly careful when packing raw food items.

After sealing, carefully check if there's any hole or mistakes in the sealing. If there are, redo it with a new bag.

Always check the product after it has been thawed. If it smells off or looks weird, don't consume it and discard it properly. Some vacuum-sealed meat will have a certain smell after it is opened. This is normal and should go away after around 30 minutes. If it still has that smell after an hour, discard it properly too.

It is good practice to label and date your vacuum-packed food. Try to consume everything in your freezer before storing more.

Vacuum Sealing Meat

Vacuum sealing red meats has a lot of benefits, even for home and domestic use. For one, it can keep the meat from going bad for really long periods of time, and two, with a lot of people now doing sous vide at home, a vacuum sealer is now a regular piece of appliance in some people's homes.

Again, try to get the freshest meat you can find. If you are not a hunter, try to look for a reputable butcher shop that sells fresh meat not flash-frozen and thawed. It will keep longer when frozen if you manage to vacuum seal it fresh.

Before you seal the red meat, check it thoroughly to see if it has discoloration or any bloodshot portions. Trim these parts out along with some of the excess fat. Quickly wash the meat under clean potable water to remove any debris or impurities and completely dry the meat with kitchen towels.

Cut the meat into smaller manageable pieces that can fit nicely in the bags and then place them relatively flat inside the bags. For steak cuts, lie them flat inside the plastic. You can stack 2 to 3 cuts of 1-inch steaks on top of each other depending on the size of your cuts and bags. For chunkier cuts, pack them in a relatively flat mass.

Meat vacuum packed for sous vide meals should be well spaced apart so all of it can cook evenly in the water. Don't stack them on top of each other if you are vacuum-packing steaks. Instead of stacking, place them side by side. The same is true with other kinds of meats like patties or fillet mignons - place them inside the bags spaced apart.

Don't forget to cut all the bones out - any sharp edges can puncture the plastic when the machine sucks the air out. If you really want to leave the bone in like you would for bone marrow steaks, make sure there aren't any sharp edges and the shapes are not that jagged. You might also want to cover the protruding bone with kitchen paper to protect the plastic.

To really make your meats last, you can add oxygen absorbers inside the bags alongside the meats before sealing them to remove all excess oxygen that can be left inside the bag. This is especially true if the meats are cut in a way where there are cavities inside, making them harder to seal.

A trick to make the meat last longer is to freeze the items before sealing. A good method is to wrap it in a freezer bag and place it side the freezer until it is completely frozen. Around 1 day or 24 hours should do it. After 24 hours, you can vacuum pack it as you normally would.

Good quality fresh meat will sometimes have liquid inside. And no matter how much you dry it with a kitchen towel, there might still be enough liquid remaining inside that can be sucked out and into the machine during the sealing process. So if you have meat that is particularly juicy, stick a kitchen towel near the opening before you seal it. The kitchen towel can absorb the excess liquid instead.

It is also a good idea to actually add seasoning to the meat before you vacuum pack it. Even a simple salt rub will do the trick. This is a great way to let the flavor permeate through the fibers of the meat, making for a tastier meal, especially if you are planning to use it for sous vide.

For raw minced meat that you made into patties: when the patties are at room temperature, they will be mushy and won't hold their shape well when under vacuum pressure. But a quick stint in the freezer for around 10 to 15 minutes after shaping will make the patty hold its shape better when the machine sucks the air out.

Vacuum Sealing Poultry

Vacuum sealing poultry, you'll find, is quite different from sealing your red meats. Red meats will mostly be chunks of meat that are already cut prettily to size. Unless you are a hunter or a butcher, you won't have to deal with ribs and cavities that much. But for poultry, since most are a lot smaller than the former, it's not strange to see butcher shops and stores selling whole poultry alongside fillets and chopped individual pieces.

Of course, you can vacuum seal your bird whole so long as your vacuum sealer can handle the size of a whole turkey. The problem is that when whole uncut poultry is vacuum-sealed, you will not be able to eliminate all the air inside, thus negating the main purpose of vacuum packing, which is to eliminate the air or oxygen inside the package. If you must insist on vacuum packing whole uncut poultry, consider adding packets of oxygen absorbers inside the bag before sealing.

A lot of information out there on the internet would tell you to fill the cavity with stuffing, but I would rather advise against it. As I said before, freezing the stuffing inside the poultry may increase the chances of contamination and spoilage even if you vacuum pack and freeze it. There will be air left inside one way or another, so it will not be a 100% perfect seal.

You can flatten the bird, though, to facilitate better airflow when sealing - this is called "spatchcocking." You would need kitchen shears for this one. With the cavity facing you, hold onto the tail and use the shears to cut at a side of the spine - around half an inch away from it. Cut in a straight line all the way from the tail to the neck. Do the same cut on the opposite side of the spine. Doing so will let you cleanly lift the spine away from the bird.

After removing the spine, spread the bird out flat as best as you can with your hands. Find the keel bone - it is at the center, white, and at the bottom of the breast bone. Make 2 cuts from the neck to the tail on either side of it. Then, using both hands, bend the rib cages away from each other until the keel bone can be clearly seen. Take this out by running your fingers under it and pulling.

To go even further, you can break the wings and the thigh off from their sockets until only the skin is left holding it together. A flat bird will go through your sealer with ease, and you won't even have to think about cavities of air inside your package anymore.

Another idea is to use an extra-large bag and shove the plastic all the way inside before sealing. This is not a foolproof method, and it will also depend on whether you have a big enough machine or not.

And last, of course, is the most obvious - butcher the bird so you can vacuum pack it in pieces.

Canning

Basics of Canning

Nonno could eat all kinds of hams and meats from his deli every day, and he would never get tired of it. But if there's one thing that he equally loves just as much, it's peaches. When I was just a kid, after school, I would raid Nonna's kitchen for canned peaches, and I would run over to our deli around the corner and sit out in the back steps. I'd eat sweet syrupy peaches with my brother and Nonno, our hands and shirts all sticky.

Nonna would give us an earful as soon as we got back, but it was all worth it. You see, those precious peaches would come to us in a crate, sent over by an aunt who lives in Romagna, Italy. In my humble opinion, they have the best, the sweetest, the most fragrant of all peaches that I have ever eaten.

Once the peaches arrive, a number would be set aside to be eaten fresh and given to my innumerable cousins, aunts, and uncles - the rest would be canned. Nonna would then set about the kitchen doing the task of canning those precious peaches that I would be ordered to "borrow" and take to our deli for a "taste test." Months after the fresh peaches were all gone, Nonna's canned peaches were just as good or even better than some of those you could buy in the local market.

You see, canning can really lengthen the shelf life of food. Much like vacuum packing, canning seals the vessel creating an airtight vacuum inside, which prevents the microbes from making contact with the food inside. But unlike vacuum packing, with canning, you make an effort to sterilize the food inside prior to sealing. There are a number of different ways on how you can do this, but sterilization by cooking the food inside the vessel in temperatures past the boiling point is the most effective, as well as adding artificial or natural preservatives inside.

For example, food with low acidities like meat, poultry, and fish needs to be sterilized at very high temperatures with the help of a pressure canner. While foods that are highly acidic, like fruits and vegetables, can be canned safely by just boiling them in water.

While some people may be averse to eating canned foods every day for fear of it lacking any nutritional value, a few studies actually suggest the opposite. Canned food is found to be richer in dietary fibers as well as vitamins when compared to frozen or even fresh food.

Tools and Equipment

Canning at home can be easy as long as you have the proper equipment and knowledge. But first, you must ensure the quality of your food before you can them. For best results, choose fresh and good quality food.

If you butcher your own meats, these should be immediately chilled and canned as soon as possible. It's also imperative that you avoid canning meats from dead or sick animals. The same is true with fish - these should be cleaned, gutted, and chilled right after catching them and should be canned within 2 days.

Fruits and vegetables reach their peak quality within 6 to 12 hours after their harvest, so it is best to can them within that time frame. Fruits need to ripen before you can them for the best results.

The basic concept of canning is this: hot air expands, and cool air shrinks. When very hot foods are poured or placed inside jars and sealed, the cooling air inside will shrink, creating a tight vacuum inside the jar. This vacuum seal, along with the high heat the food has been and will be subjected to after sealing, is the reason why canning works. Coupled with the ease of how it is done and the long storage life makes canning widely practiced today, whether it be commercially - in massive canning factories - or from the comfort of your own home.

There are a couple of different methods on how you can approach canning for your own home, and through the years, some have been proven more effective than others. For instance, open kettle canning and oven canning are now deemed dangerous because of safety reasons. On open kettle canning, even though the food is boiling when poured into the jar, that heat alone is not enough to kill all bacteria, mold, and yeast that can get into the jar before it gets sealed. Furthermore, just the heat from the food alone will not be enough to kill all contaminants.

The proper way is to let the jar undergo pressure canning or be processed in a boiling water canner. This will not only eliminate all contaminants and lower the chances of spoilage but also create a tighter vacuum seal. The same goes with oven canning. The heat inside the oven cannot match the heat generated in pressure canning or even in a hot boiling water canner. Even if you bump up your oven's internal temperature to 240°F, it will not heat up the inside of the jar to the same temperature.

Oven canning is also problematic for home canning, where glass jars are mainly used. Placing these glass jars in the oven poses an even greater risk for your safety as the glass can shatter or explode inside the oven.

And so we have hot packing and raw packing. Between these two, hot packing is the recommended method if you plan to use a boiling water canner. This is when food is boiled in very high heat for 2 to 5 minutes and then transferred into the jars immediately. With raw packing, on the other hand, the jars are filled with prepared and unheated foods and then closed. When adding syrup, water, or juice inside the jars, keep in mind that they should also undergo the same treatment as the food itself: heated to boiling. The jars are then closed tightly and processed in a boiling water canner for 30 minutes to 60 minutes or for 60 minutes to 100 minutes for pressure canners.

You can buy most home canning equipment easily. It is recommended to use threaded mason jars with wide mouths and self-sealing lids. These glass jars are favored for home canning as they are reusable and would only need a new lid each time; you'll also find that they are cheaper than metal canisters. Contrary to popular belief, these mason jars do not break easily as long as you handle them with proper care. Commercial mayonnaise and salad dressing jars can also be used with new lids, but these jars might be more prone to leakage and breakage as the glass has a tendency to weaken over time. Lids for canning should only be bought and stocked as you need them; storing them for years unused may cause the lid to malfunction.

Before canning, good hygiene is essential: clean and disinfect everything you will be using before you start. The jars need to be sterilized too by boiling them in water for 10 minutes or more and then dried. Prepare items - food that is cut and peeled should be submerged in an ascorbic acid solution to prevent browning.

On canners, there are two main types that are mainly used for home canning. As I mentioned above, these are **boiling water canners** and **pressure canners.** These come big enough that they can hold several glass jars at once - around 7 or 8 jars depending on the size of the jars. Both come with a handy rack where you can place your jars for easier lifting and lowering. I would tell beginners to actually try with a boiling water canner first before moving on to the pressure canners. Pressure canners, in general, would need more experience to work as it has more steps and more accessories with it. But if you are planning to can low acid foods like meat, fish, and poultry, then a pressure canner is the only way to go.

Made of porcelain or aluminum steel bodies, **boiling water canners** also come with racks and fitted lids. At the same time, these should be tall enough that when sealed jars are lowered, the tops are covered by about 1 inch of water. In preparation, these canners should be filled halfway with clean water and set to boil at 140°F for foods that are raw packed and 180°F for hot packed foods. Leave enough headspace between the lid and the food inside so the air will have enough space to expand and contract. When the jars are ready, lower them into the boiling water carefully, keeping them level to avoid spilling food over the sealing area of the jar.

Top it off with more boiling water as needed to fully submerge the jars - the water level should always be 1 inch above the tops of the jar; however, if the processing time requires you to boil the jars for more than 30 minutes, the water level should always be 2 inches above the jars. If the water level drops down at any time during the boiling process, add more boiling water to bring it back up. Keep the canner covered and the water inside on a constant rolling boil during the entire process to kill off all the bacteria and contaminants that may spoil your food. If, at any time, the boiling stops, you would need to restart the boiling process again.

After the boiling process, let the jars rest inside the canner for 5 minutes before taking them out. Leave the jars to cool to room temperature before storing them - around 12 to 24 hours.

Pressure canners have come far from thick-walled kettles - they are now lightweight and have thinner bodies. The pressure will not kill off the microorganisms, but the high internal temperature generated inside the canner will. You must also take into account the altitude of your current location. Studies have found that the internal temperatures inside pressure canners will be lower at higher altitudes, so the pressure inside the canners must be adjusted to the right altitude range. Air trapped inside the canner can also lower the internal temperature significantly, so always remember to release or vent the air for 10 minutes before you can go about pressurizing the canner.

Pressure canners are more high maintenance than the above boiling water canners. For example, the lid gasket should be cleaned and handled carefully. Damaged or dried gaskets will lead to steam leaks during pressurization that can lead to unsafe food.

To use a pressure canner is relatively simple - the process doesn't differ that much from the boiling water canner except for a few things. Unlike boiling water canners, jars shouldn't be submerged fully in water. Just add 2 to 3 inches of hot water into the canner and slowly and carefully lower the jars. Also, avoid tilting the jars to avoid spilling food on the jar lid.

Fasten the canner lid and set the heat to the highest setting while leaving the vent port open. Let the steam come out from the port continuously for 10 minutes before placing the weight onto the vent port. By placing the weight on the vent port, the canner will be pressurized within 3 to 5 minutes.

Start timing the process when the weight starts to

jiggle around. Next, you'll need to watch for constant pressure in heat. Follow the canner's manufacturer instructions to know how to maintain the right pressure inside the canner. If the pressure goes down during the middle of the canning process, you will need to restart the whole process again from the beginning.

When the process is complete, carefully take the canner off the heat and let it cool down and allow it to depressurize by itself. Never try to force the pressure canner to cool down by dunking it in water, or worse, an ice bath. It might cause seal failures in your jars inside and might cause the canner walls to warp, rendering them useless. When the canner is finally depressurized, take off the weight and open the vent port and wait for another 10 minutes before opening it and taking the canner lid off. Be careful about the steam - open the lid away from you as the steam can cause burns. Lift the jars out of the canner and let them cool to room temperature undisturbed for 12 to 24 hours before storing.

Procedure and Preparation

Red meats and poultry can be canned using a pressure

canner, and you can either use the hot packing method or the raw packing method. For raw packing, raw cuts of meat and poultry should be packed into the jars with around 1 teaspoon of salt for every quart.

Hot packing, on the other hand, will require your meats and poultry to be cooked until they are 70% done, packed into a jar with also a teaspoon of salt for every quart. For both methods, remember to leave 1 inch of headspace between the tops of your meat and poultry and the lid of the jar.

Cut the produce up, so they fit inside the jar. Trim the excess fat from wild game, but add pork fat to leaner cuts of meat like venison. The pork fat, in this case, adds more flavor and also helps with the preservation process.

Meanwhile, to remove the strong gamey smell from wild meats, age the meats at 40°F or lower for 2 to 3 days. Afterward, soak the meats in a brine solution - 1 tablespoon of salt to a quart of potable water - for an hour and rinse well before packing the meats in a jar.

The processing times when you are pressure canning

the meats will vary depending on the way the meat and poultry are cut and the method you used when you packed them in. Below is a helpful guide that can tell you how long you should process your jars inside the canner.

Meats

(beef, lamb, pork, veal, and venison)

Minced meat or smaller chops of meat	pint	Packed hot	75 minutes
Minced meat or smaller chops of meat	quart	Packed hot	90 minutes
Chunks or strips	pint	packed raw or hot	75 minutes
Chunks or strips	quart	packed raw or hot	90 minutes

Poultry

(chicken, duck, and goose)

Without bones	pint	Packed raw	75 minutes
Without bones	quart	Packed raw	90 minutes
With bones	pint	Packed hot	65 minutes
With bones	quart	Packed hot	75 minutes

A Word On Pickling

When people hear the word pickles, pickled cucumber comes first in mind. But before the prevalence of ice and refrigeration, pickled meat was a thing.

Now, pickling is said to contain probiotics as pickling means fermenting in brine or vinegar; thus, this is our answer to the various fermented vegetables all over Asia.

Today it would be harder to find pickled meat - just the thought alone might send shivers down some people's spine, like meat jelly domes. But unlike canning, pickling will rely on the brine solution or the vinegar to actually preserve the food.

The vinegar alone is highly acidic and will be able to kill off most contaminants. To pickle, the food or meat is placed inside the jars with the pickling brine or vinegar and sealed. It will not undergo any additional canning process like pressure canning or boiling water canning.

Curing

Why Cure Meats?

Most of the time, curing and smoking work together to give the meat more complex and deeper notes of flavor. But a lot of people don't realize that curing by itself can lend absolutely wonderful flavor profiles to meat.

When you cure meat in preparation for smoking, you are preparing the meat to take on the added taste, flavor, as well as tenderness you can only achieve in a smoker. Meanwhile, when you cure meat as a single process, you are going to end up with dry-cured meat, like those hams we sell in our deli.

To dry cure meats, the meat is rubbed and coated with a salt mixture. It is sometimes then wrapped in cheesecloth and left to dry in a temperature and humidity-controlled room. But in the old days, these meats would be left to cure in caves or in cellars to be naturally coated with mold, like how they still do for some of the specialty hams we have in Italy. And you cannot deny that Italy comes up with some really good hams.

In dry curing, the salt rubbed all over the meat will help dry it out through osmosis. Salt is then dispersed throughout the cell structures of the meat, which naturally will make the meat salty enough to be inhospitable to bacteria and fungi that can cause spoilage.

However, in wet curing, meat is left submerged in a salty brine - which should have a 20% salinity to work. It works the same as dry curing - salt will penetrate through the cells walls and make the meat inhospitable to bacteria and fungi.

Before, curing meat was a way to extend the shelf life of food as a means to store food items for winters or times of need. Now, it's done for the wonderful flavors it can lend to meats. Chefs would cure meats using different brines and dry rubs flavored with different spices and ingredients to add flavor to the meat.

If some people may be averse to trying out cured meats in fear of all the sodium that's being introduced to the meat, studies show that cured meats would only retain around 1% of the salt that was introduced to them.

Dry Curing

All methods for curing are salt-based - the only difference is that on dry curing, a dry rub of salt, spices, and ingredients is rubbed into the meat instead of soaking the meat in brine. Dry curing is perfect for meats that will not undergo smoking afterward.

Dry-cured meat like the Spanish and Italian hams won't be easy to replicate as those do not rely only on the curing process to add distinct flavors to the meat. A lot of factors can play major roles in how these hams taste. The diet and breed of the animal, the altitude, the location where the curing takes place, and even the type of mold play an important role. Instead, what we have here in the book is a simple breakdown of the basic curing process, which will leave more room for you to tweak and make it your own.

To create your own curing rub, there are four major ingredients that we will be using as the base. There are many ready-made curing rubs that you can find in stores and online, so do not worry if you do not want to make your own.

Let's start with salt as it is the most readily available in all homes. What salt does is draw out enough moisture from the meat and raise the salinity enough so that the meat is rendered inhospitable for bacterial growth that can cause spoilage.

Another item that you can readily find in your home and can also be used alongside salt is sugar. By adding sugar, you are balancing out the saltiness and, at the same time, adding flavor.

Curing salts or sodium nitrate is also called pink salt and can be used separately for dry curing. This salt is colored an unnaturally pink hue, so it's not mistaken for regular salt. Ingesting this in high amounts can be toxic. So be careful with the amount of curing salt you use to cure your meat. Like normal table salt, pink salt stops bacterial growth as well as giving the meat that unmistakable red hue that all meats cured with sodium nitrate has.

Lastly, we have the spices. You can have a go with the different types of spices you would want to mix in your curing rub. For inspiration, here are some of the more popular spices that are used in curing rubs:

Chili powder

Onion powder

Paprika

Bay leaves

Star anise

Cumin

Cloves

Mustard

On choosing meats, any piece of red meat like beef, pork, turkey, or even game meat will do nicely. However, some cuts will do better than others. What you are looking for is a sub-primal or a large muscle cut of meat. Look for cuts that have the bone in and have layers of fat (for that extra flavor), like loins - pork loin, sirloin, striploin - briskets, ribeye, and hindquarters, or even pork belly. Even though you will be trimming a lot of the fat outside, layers of it marbling the meat inside and covering your meat will help your meat stay moist throughout the process.

To start dry curing, prepare your meat by trimming off the excess fats and cutting out protrusions. It's good if the shape of the meat is one whole mass without any bits sticking out, so everything is equally flavored. This is especially true if you plan to smoke it afterward. Trim the fat but don't remove it altogether. Leave an even layer of fat coating your meat. Good dry-cured meat should give out a nice sheen of fat that melts on your hand when touched.

Mix your salt rub and massage it all over the meat, making sure you get all the nooks and crannies. If the meat has a thicker layer of fat on it, poke or stab it with a fork to help the salt mixture penetrate deeper into the meat. After rubbing it all in, sprinkle another layer of the salt mixture over the meat to completely cover it.

When curing the meat at home, place the salt-covered meat in a tray and weigh it down with something heavy on top to help press the curing mixture into the meat. A pan or another tray with something heavy on top works. Just remember to leave enough room around the meat to let it breathe. Place the meat inside the refrigerator and leave it untouched for around 10 days. Afterward, rinse the salt off it with cold potable water and then pat it dry with a kitchen towel.

There is another sub-type of dry curing we call the equilibrium curing, which is perfect for home curing, especially for beginners who already have a vacuum sealer on hand. For this type of dry curing, you must choose a cut of meat that you'll have no problem fitting inside your bag. For the amount of salt, multiply the weight of the meat by 0.025 - basically 2.5% of the meat's weight. So if you have a 500g cut of meat, you will need 12.5 g of salt.

Next, prepare the meat and the salt mix like you would do in normal dry curing. Afterward, coat the meat with the salt mix and place it inside a bag for vacuum packing. Vacuum packing is advised, but a normal freezer bag can still work - you just need to remove almost all the air from the bag.

Place the vacuum-sealed bag inside the refrigerator and allow it to cure untouched. You will find that water will seep out of the meat, but it's normal - just let it be as this is part of the process. You can leave it to cure this way for months on end, but the minimum amount of time for it to cure is 5 days.

Wet Curing/Brine Curing

We've talked a lot about brining before in freezing fish

and when canning meats. That's because salt can really help preserve food, and brining is an easy and cheap way to prevent bacteria from spoiling your food. The difference is that with wet curing, the meat is soaked in a salt solution for at least 12 hours instead of just a few minutes or hours. That is why it is best to choose meats that are leaner, with more muscles than what you would choose for dry curing.

Meats that are best for wet curing are the ones that have less moisture content in them and tend to lose it as well during cooking. Soaking them in a brine solution will help hold the moisture inside the meat, giving you a juicier result. As always, fresh meat should be used, and never use any meat that has already been treated with pink salt.

To wet cure the meat, you will need a brine. It is quite similar to dry curing but with added water. For a basic recipe, all you need is to add 1 cup of salt to 2 cups of water and ¼ cup of sugar in a pot. Heat and stir well. When everything is dissolved, turn off the heat and let it come to room temperature. Add 2 more cups of clean potable water and store covered in a fridge until you are ready to use it.

To tweak your brine solution, you can choose to add other ingredients and spices. Be careful about how many extra ingredients you add. The resulting brine solution must have 20% salinity in order for it to work, so if you're not sure about the salinity of your brine solution, it is better to buy a salinometer. That said, here are some of the more popular ingredients you can add to your brine solution:

Honey

Herbs

Citrus zest or juice

Buttermilk

Ginger

Garlic

Molasses

Whiskey or beer

Apple cider

When your brine is chilling in the fridge, it is time to prepare your meat for wet curing. If there is any, trim the meat of fat or even out the distribution of it across the surface of your meat. Also, cut out any protrusions. We want a smooth whole chunk of meat so everything will be flavored equally in the end.

In a resealable container or a freezer bag, place the meat inside along with the brine solution. If you are using a container, make sure the meat is well submerged in the solution with no bits poking out of the surface. In freezer bags, remember to leave enough room so you can still close it and to turn it once a day so every surface of the meat can come in contact with the solution.

For every pound of meat, it is recommended to cure the meat in the brine solution for at least 12 hours in the fridge. This will give your meat enough time to absorb all the flavors and salt in the brine. If you have a huge chunk of meat and will want or need to cure it for more than 7 days, change the brine solution on the 7th day and shove it back into the fridge.

When the meat is done curing, rinse it in cold potable water to remove all the excess salt and pat dry with a kitchen towel. Place it back inside the fridge wrapped in cheesecloth until you are ready to use it.

Storage

Like all the other methods of food preservation, curing can definitely preserve meat for long-term storage but not preserve it to the point that it is incorruptible. At the very least, you can extend its shelf life for months, sometimes years, but it can even go as short as days. So here's a handy list you can copy out and tack on your fridge door for reference.

Meat	State	Room temperature	Fridge	Freezer
Pepperoni	unopened	6 weeks	9 weeks	1 year

Pepperoni	opened	-	3 weeks	4 weeks
Pork (salami-hard/ham)	Unopened (vacuum sealed)	4 weeks	8 weeks	3 months
Pork (salami-hard/ham)	opened	3 weeks	5 weeks	3 months
Pancetta	unopened	-	5 weeks	1 year
Pancetta	opened	-	3 weeks	-
Prosciutto	unopened	-	5 weeks	1 year
Prosciutto	opened	-	3 weeks	-
Chorizo	Wrapped in cloth	-	6 weeks	8 weeks
Poultry	unopened	-	2 weeks	1 year

Fish (lightly cured)	unopened	-	2 weeks	3 months
Fish (highly cured like salted cod or salmon)	unopened	-	1 year or more	1 year or more

As always, there are exceptions; there are some methods of curing that can leave meat stable enough that it can be left at room temperature for really long periods without any signs of spoilage. For this to happen, the meat must undergo dehydration as well as curing. Both make sure that the meat is absolutely inhospitable to bacteria. There are limited meat products that are shelf-stable - an excellent example of this is jerky.

Smoking

Reasons to Smoke Meat

Ah, smoking - we have our own smoker out back in the deli. Nonno rigged it up decades ago out of an old barrel for smoking the pancetta Nonna would need to make our dinner. But my father expanded it into a small brick shed where we can smoke a couple more racks of beef and pork at the same time to sell in the store - much to Nonno's chagrin. You see, we people from the Mediterranean have a love affair more so with curing than of smoking. But anyway, the best thing that comes out of that smoker is pastrami that we make for our friendly neighborhood food truck.

I'm sure you have seen bottles of liquid smoke as you go around in stores. They are marketed as an easier alternative in order to bring that smokey flavor into dishes. It will definitely bring more flavor to the food by mimicking the flavor of smoked meats, but it would not lend that preserving effect to it. It is a modern invention to make our lives easier, as smoking food, you will learn later, is much harder than sprinkling seasoning over your brisket.

As a preservation tool, I wouldn't recommend smoking by itself. Even though smoking has its benefits, such as being antimicrobial and also an antioxidant, by itself, it is not enough to preserve the meat. It doesn't have the means to penetrate far into the center of the cut. Therefore, it is often paired up with other forms of food preservation, such as dehydration or curing. So why do we smoke meat? It's an extra step we take to preserve the meat. And not only that, anyone who eats pastrami, smoked pancetta, or smoked pulled pork BBQ can swear by the complex flavors smoking can give to meat. It can really enhance the flavor of the meat as well as make it really soft, especially when you cook it via smoking.

For food preservation, the doubled method of smoking and salt curing is especially effective for fish that can be categorized as oily. Smoking, in this case, with its antioxidant properties, can stop the surface fat from becoming rancid faster. It can also delay the contact of the inside fat from oxygen that can hasten spoilage. And so, with fish that is heavily salt-cured and smoked for a really long time, it can be stored at room temperature for months without spoilage. Another example is katsuobushi from Japan. Boiled, smoked, dried, and fermented, these are proclaimed as one of the hardest foods in the world and will keep at room temperature indefinitely.

Smoking is done in an enclosed space with hardwood chips smoldering in low heat for a very long time. There are basically 2 types of smoking that you can do. One is cold smoking which will only envelope the meat with the flavor and aroma of smoke without cooking or preserving it. Even though cold smoking will only reach temperatures as low as 70°F, it will still be enough to remove excess moisture from the meat but not enough to dehydrate it. It is usually done in a dual-chambered smoker - the smoking chamber is separate from the chamber where the wood chips and the fire is. Since cold smoking will not cook the meat, it is highly advisable to cook it in another way before or after the smoking process to make it safe to consume.

The second type is hot smoking. With this type of smoking, temperatures can go from 150°F up to 220°F and can cook any meat for you whether they are cured or not. It can also dehydrate the meat if you leave it in the smoker for longer periods of time. For meat that is falling off the bone, or you can easily pull it apart with just a spoon, I would recommend smoking it for longer times in lower temperatures. You'll find that the resulting meat will be more tender and succulent.

Next, we need to talk about the meats that are great for smoking. Basically, any meat can benefit from the deeper flavor smoking gives. But the bigger cuts will definitely do better inside the smoker, especially if they have a nice marbling of fat on and in them. In slow smoking, the fats melt slowly and will be giving the meat that fall-off-the-bone moment that everyone wants. Here are some cuts that will be good for smoking:

Pork roast

Pork shoulder

Pork butt

Whole poultry (chicken or turkey)

Ribs

Beef brisket

Prime rib

Tools and Equipment

To start smoking meat at home, the first thing you need would be the smokers themselves. Smokers come in different sizes and shapes, you can buy commercially made ones, or you can make something out of barrels as Nonno did. Smoking is essentially hanging or placing meat on a rack with a smoldering pile of slow-burning wood underneath it. You can easily make your own smoker from an electric griddle or a small metal bucket with charcoal and terracotta pots. You can even make use of your grill at home to smoke meats if you know what to do.

The new and improved version we use at the deli is the DIY kind. My father is quite the handyman - he even made a brick oven in our backyard one summer. But for those who do not want the hassle of building their own smoker, commercially available smokers now come in a large range of sizes and come fueled with either wood, gas, electricity, and even charcoal.

Wood or fire smokers are basic and have been used for centuries. These will give you a deeper, more woody flavor. But since you are dealing with naked fire, it will need constant tending and attention - definitely not for beginners as it will take longer to master temperature control with these smokers.

Pellet smokers also use wood, in a sense. The difference is that these make use of condensed wooden pellets instead, thus making it easier to control the temperature when compared to the old-school wood smoker. Although it still makes use of wood, the flavor will be slightly different, but it will definitely give the meat more flavor than the electric or gas smokers.

Making use of charcoal is another old way of smoking meat. It will give your meat a different flavor when compared to wood smokers. It's not by any means inferior to wood smoke - it's just different and will ultimately depend on a person's preferences. And like fire, it will be hard to maintain the temperature with these smokers and will need constant tending - and fanning for those really old-school charcoal smokers. It's definitely not recommended for beginners.

Electric smokers are a more recent invention. It will still give you that woody flavor - although on the lighter side - as it makes use of heated coils to burn wood chips. These will come with dials for easy temperature controls, making them great for beginners.

Propane smokers are a cross between electric and older wood smokers. Since it is gas-fueled, the flame is easier to control, making it good for beginners too. But if you have a good charcoal grill at home, I would actually recommend that you just use that one instead of buying your own smoker. If you asked me, unless you are planning to start a small business selling smoked meat, I would actually tell you to make use of your grill or make your own small smoker yourself.

If you want to test out smoking in your backyard first, try smoking the meat with charcoal or a gas grill. Let's start with the charcoal grill first since it is more common, and the setup is simple enough.

Start your grill as you normally would by loading it up with charcoal but only on one side of the grill. On the opposite side of the pile of charcoal, place a drip tray to catch the juices from the meat. Fire up the grill and once the coals are hot enough, place wood chips on top of the glowing coals. Once the wood starts smoking, place the meat on the grill above the drip tray and close the lid of the grill. Remember to leave a small gap open for ventilation.

Gas grills are another common thing in backyards, and they can also be used to smoke meats. The setup is a bit different from the charcoal grills. First, you would need to open all the burners on high to preheat your grill for about 20 minutes. After 20 minutes, close all burners except for one side. On the side with naked flames, place the wood chips in a robust metal tray and place them directly on the burners. On the opposite side, where the burners are off, place the meat. When the wood starts smoking, close the grill lid but leave a small gap for ventilation.

For a quick, small, and portable smoker, you can rummage around out back and look for a large terracotta pot that you're not using (or just buy one at a flea market). A terracotta smoker is easy to assemble and will only need a few materials before you can start smoking your first meat.

First, you would need a small electric hot plate. It should be small enough to fit inside the clay pot you will be using. Choose one that is 1,000 watts or more.

Next, you will need a clay pot that is tall and large enough to hold the hot plate, the grill, and the meat inside comfortably. It will also need a cover that can keep the smoke in. It doesn't need to be an airtight lid. In fact, the clay pot or another pot can be used as lids.

You would also need a grill that can sit inside the clay pot. It should sit around ¾ from the bottom. The grill or the meat shouldn't touch the hot plate or even the wood chips that you are going to place on top of the hot plate. And finally, use heat-resistant gloves for handling the pots.

For this smoker to work, you would need to drill a hole or enlarge the normally existing hole on the bottom of the pot to let the electrical cord and plug pass through easily. Be careful when drilling - pots will have a tendency to crack if drilled incorrectly. Insert the hot plate inside the pot and feed the plug and cord out through the hole. The hot plate should sit snugly on the bottom.

Place the whole pot on top of some bricks or patio blocks to elevate it from the ground - remember to do this outside in the open air. This would help stop the hot plate from overheating. Make sure the pot and its supports are sitting on level ground. Add wood chips in a metal pan directly on top of the hot plate and insert the grill inside the pot. Leave enough space between the wood chips and the grill. Place the meat in, cover the pot, and you are ready to start smoking.

Now, you might be wondering why I'm telling you not to close the lids entirely and to leave a small gap for ventilation. When smoking meats, the smoke should move around and should be allowed to escape. This ventilation is called a smoke flow, and a small gap left open in the grill or in your pot will guarantee good smoking to the meat. A stagnant smoke inside a smoker will have unwanted results. A tightly closed smoker with no smoke escaping will mean that the smoke will accumulate faster inside, and the internal temperatures will rise to leave you with charred and ashy remnants of meat.

Now let's talk about the types of wood. The type of wood and the cut of meat you end up smoking will determine the quality and the flavor of your end product. You will find that professional smokers will have their own recipe when it comes to picking the types of wood they use. This is because the type of wood you end up using is also a factor if you want tender and juicy smoked meat. The type of wood is totally different from the size and shape of the wood, which we will talk about later.

That said, you will want to use wood that is slow-burning and can produce a good smolder. Steer clear from softwoods as they have a lot more sap and essential oils. When burned, softwoods will give off a pungent and thick smoke that you don't want anywhere near the meat. Therefore, what you are looking for is hardwood. Examples of good hardwoods that you can use are apples, cherry, or alder. You are also not limited to one kind, as you can use different types of wood at the same time to create a unique flavor profile. Play around with pairing a deeper tasting wood with something fruity like oak and apple.

Different types of wood work well with different types of meat. For example, when smoking poultry and fish, the lighter and sweeter woods like apple and cherry would pair better as these can easily absorb more flavor from the smoke. Whereas the heavier, stronger-smelling woods like walnut and mesquite work best with beef and pork, which tend to take longer for the smoke to lend its flavor.

Deeper or mellow flavors:

Walnut- Great for beef and pork

Pecan - Fruity flavor; hickory like; mellow; Great for beef, pork, and chicken

Peach- Great for chicken and pork

Oak - Mesquite-like but mellower; subtle flavor; Great for long periods of smoking; Great for beef, pork, chicken, and seafood

Pear - Great for chicken and pork

Maple - Subtle and sweet; mellow; Great for chicken

Mesquite - Tangy flavor; Will be pungent after long periods of smoking; Great for beef and pork

Mulberry - Great for pork, poultry, and seafood

Hickory - Great with anything that is meant to be broiled or barbequed; Great for beef, pork, ribs, and bacon; Sweet and light flavor

Birch - Delicate tasting smoke, sweet; Great for pork, chicken, lamb, and seafood

Apple - Fruity and sweet smoke; Great for poultry, pork, and seafood

Alder - Mild flavor; Great for pork, seafood, and chicken

Cherry - Fruity and sweet, tart aftertaste; Great for beef, pork, chicken, and seafood

Now you decide what size and shape of wood you will be using. The biggest are **wood chunks**. Most big commercial smokers use larger chunks of wood as these will last longer and can smoke the meat for hours and days at a time. **Wood chips** are smaller and will last shorter than wood chunks. If you only want to smoke the meat for a few hours, wood chips will work fine. The smallest of the bunch are **pellets**. Smoker pellets can burn off rather quickly and are only designed to be used with pellet smokers. When using pellet smokers, the pellets can burn slower, making them easier to control. But still, pellet smokers can only smoke the meats for even shorter periods than wood chips, so it is best used when you only want to add a light level of smokiness to the meat.

You can also soak the wood if you want to. It's not imperative that you should, but dry wood will burn much quicker than wet wood. If you are going to soak the wood, remember to drain them properly before you place them in your smoker. Doing so will lengthen the burn time as well as the smolder. Bigger sizes like chunks would need to soak for an hour, while chips need only soak for 30 minutes. Another thing you can try is to soak the wood in beer or juice. This will give an extra kick to the flavor of the smoked meat. To add even more complex flavors, try throwing in some dried herbs and spices in with the wood.

To control the smoke, regulate the amount of moisture and oxygen inside your smoker. More moisture in the wood will make it burn longer and produce more smoke. More oxygen inside the smoker means bigger flames which will eat up the fuel and the wood faster.

Procedure

Like a good cast iron pan, you need to season a smoker

first before you can start using it. For smokers, we call this step curing. To cure the smoker, try getting the temperature to go as high as 390°F. Once it reaches that temperature, drop it to 220°F and let it continue to smoke for 2 hours or more. Doing it like this will remove the contaminants and other smells in the smoker as well as season it, so it is ready for the meat.

Next, get your meats and the wood ready. Cured meats should be cured beforehand; otherwise, coat them with a dry rub or marinades at this stage. Frozen and chilled meats should be thawed to room temperature. Fire up the smoker and let it heat up for 30 minutes. Leave the vents, or the lid open a bit to let a small amount of smoke out. If you have a laser thermometer, you can go ahead and check the internal temperatures. For good smoking, the temperatures inside should reach 200°F but never past 250°F. Once the smoker reaches the optimal temperature, you can then add the wood chips, pellets, or chunks in.

Lower the internal temperature of the smoker by cutting off the oxygen inside. You can do this by closing the vents a bit at a time or by adjusting the lid of the smoker. Reducing the oxygen inside the smoker will make more smoke inside.

Fill up a metal tray or pan with a shallow layer of water and place it inside, nearer to the fire and wood chips. This is to introduce water vapor inside and is useful if you plan to cook the meat while it is smoking. The water vapor will ensure the meat cooks evenly. Be careful not to overfill the pan. The more water you have inside, the lower the internal temperatures will get, so make sure the water level is only half an inch maximum. And as with soaking the wood with beer or juice, instead of plain water, you can also use beer and juice on the pan. Fruit juices like pineapple and apples are best paired with poultry.

You can now place the meat inside the smoker or on top of the grill. You are going to cook the meat using indirect heat, so the whole process will be a lot slower - 500g of meat will mean it needs to smoke for 1 hour or 1 ½ hours. This is why it is best to keep the heat low and the temperature steady all throughout the smoking process. Close the lid until there is a small gap and leave it alone. If you want juicier meat, wrap it in foil for a third of the overall smoking time. Some professional smokers will frown upon this as they leave the meat uncovered the whole time, but smoking for long periods of time can dehydrate the meat too.

So, to ensure juicy and succulent meat, divide the smoking time into 3 unequal parts. Leave the meat uncovered for the first part - that is half the entire smoking time- and wrapped in foil for the 2nd. That is a third of the entire smoking time. Then, leave unwrapped again for the final stretch. For example, if the smoking time is 2 hours, the first hour will have the meat smoking uncovered, then 40 minutes wrapped in foil. The last 20 minutes will be uncovered.

Do not be tempted to open the smoker to check on the meat. Opening and closing the smoker over and over again will decrease the internal temperature and dissipate the smoke - not to mention that it will only make for a longer smoking time. Only open the grill or the smoker if you need to add more wood chips or add more fuel. Minimize opening and closing it to once per hour.

You also won't need to rotate the meat inside the smoker. If you have good smoke flow inside the smoker, you will not need to rotate or flip the meat. Again, you will be cooking using indirect heat; there is no reason why you would need to flip or rotate it during smoking. Unless you have a huge smoker with racks upon racks of meat smoking at the same time, you don't need to touch the meat again once you put it in. Some will want to coat the meat with marinade or sauce while it is smoking, but I would recommend you do that in the last 20 minutes or even after the whole process is done. If you choose to add sauce after the meat is done, put it back in the smoker as soon as it is coated with sauce and allow the meat to smoke again for another 15 minutes. The added time in the smoker will allow the flavors in the sauce to be layered and baked on top.

If you are worried that the meat is not cooking inside the smoker, fret not - once you've checked the smoker's internal temperature in the beginning and refrained from opening and closing the lid, the internal temperatures should be the same all throughout the process. And once you smoke the meat for more than 2 hours, there is little chance that the meat will come out uncooked.

Dehydrating

Dehydrating Basics

Dehydration is the act of food preservation where food is dehydrated or desiccated to stop spoilage and bacterial growth. It is a method of food preservation that our cave-dwelling ancestors used to stay alive and is therefore also the oldest method that's amazingly still used today. Traditionally, moisture from the food is removed through various natural means like sun drying, air drying, and even smoking, when done for weeks and months at a time. All over the world, people in different countries have their own native and traditional food that is still intrinsically tied to dehydration, from the dried and fermented sharks in Greenland to dried and smoked jerky that can last for years and even the infamous rock-hard *katsuobushi* in Japan. Everywhere you look, from traditional and exotic markets to the humdrum groceries and neighborhood delis, dried food products are still widely enjoyed today.

So why do we dehydrate food? First of all, it is the easiest way you can preserve food products. For the most basic types of dehydration, you don't need any equipment - just the sun and air will be enough. And it works well with almost any type of food, from sun-dried meats of long gone cavemen to dried persimmons strung out to dry in colorful garlands in the rural towns of East Asia.

Throughout history, the process of dehydration has branched out and evolved to different methods, but the basics are the same. Moisture is removed through evaporation by applying or exposing the food item to heat, wind, or both. The lack of moisture in the food will, in turn, inhibit bacterial growth, thereby prolonging the shelf life of products.

Another reason why people choose to dehydrate their food is for easier and more convenient storage when traveling. Dehydrated food will weigh much less than normal food, therefore, making it easier to bring more foodstuff to camping, bunkers, traps, or even rock climbing. By drying out liquids to powdered forms - like eggs and milk - you can also prolong the shelf life of easily perishable products for long-term travel or storage.

Others dry their food to change the texture and flavor of the item. Drying out food items has a tendency to intensify flavors - like shiitake mushrooms. It can also add complex flavors to food when combined with other forms of preservation like curing.

Now, drying methods are not only limited to the power of the sun and the wind. The modern era has given us other quicker and more reliable methods on how we can dehydrate our food. Most common right now are home food dehydrators, but there is also microwave-vacuum drying, bed dryers, spray drying, and combined thermal hybrid drying. We in the deli choose to dry our meats by smoking them or drying them out by the sun. Nonno and I are convinced that these two methods impart different flavors to the meat. My father begs to disagree, though!

Tools and Equipment

Since this book is teaching you how to preserve food in the comfort of your own home, we are going to talk about food dehydrators for home use. These kitchen appliances have been popping up in kitchens all over the world for quite a while now. Before, dehydrating food at home feels like something a grandmother would do, but with this appliance, drying food is as easy as popping food into the microwave.

And like a microwave, the variety may make it harder to choose the right one. Modern home dehydrators are either made with plastic or metal and glass. They have heating elements, and fans inside that can blow hot air around to dry out food. With front loading dehydrators, the more expensive one of the two types, the fans and the heating elements, are located at the back and will blow the hot air across the trays inside.

This will normally have a glass window for you to see if you are done with the drying process. And since these are made of glass and metal, the trays are most likely dishwasher safe. If this sounds so much like a convection oven, that's because, yes, it is like a convection oven in a sense. In fact, if you have a convection oven at home, you don't need a standalone dehydrator. The convection oven can do dehydration for you.

Stackable dehydrators are another type. These are more likely made of BPA-free plastic, which might not be the most dishwasher-safe material. Made of stacks of racks that remind me of bamboo steamers, stackable dehydrators have fans and heating elements located at the top and bottom of the appliance and will blow hot air through the racks in a column. Less expensive than the first, these usually come with the issue of uneven drying. Owners of stackable dehydrators find that they might need to rotate the stacks to achieve even drying. But the stackable feature also means that you can add and subtract stacks to customize the drying process. Take away what is done and leave the rest to continue drying.

Another important thing to consider is temperature control. Most dehydrators should come with a temperature controller, but some might not. A dehydrator without it will make it difficult to adjust the heat for a perfect, even drying. You might as well stick with sun drying if you cannot control the temperature.

Procedure

Like all the other methods of food prep we have discussed above, sterilization and hygiene should come as second nature when it comes to food preparation. Raw meats should be handled with care and kept separate from cooked meats to avoid contamination. Utensils, equipment, and countertops should always be kept clean and dry. Hands should be washed and dried often after handling food items - or better yet, wear gloves.

It is always better to be extra careful when handling or prepping large amounts of food to prevent accidental contamination that may lead to spoilage. In general, meat should be cooked first before it is processed for drying, but only select the freshest meat for this process. Choose to dry leaner cuts of meat with less fat. The leaner the cut, the longer it will keep in storage. Fatty meats, when dried, will become rancid faster than you think. So it's best to avoid them. For example, duck and goose meats will not do well dried because of it's higher fat content.

And whether you are sun-drying them or using the dehydrator, thinner slices will always work better and dry faster than whole chunks of meat. So slice the meat into slivers and use a mandoline on the fruits.

Drying food is a slow process, although it is much faster now with modern dehydrators. You shouldn't spend the whole time looking at it while it does its job like you would with a microwave. Bumping up the temperature will not make it dry out any faster. In any case, it will form a hard shell where the outside is perfectly dried but with the moisture still trapped inside. A slow and steady drying process will ensure that the food is dried out evenly. To make sure the food is not case-hardened, test one out before storage by slicing or cutting it in half to check the state inside.

For poultry, boil them first - or better yet, cook them in a pressure cooker for the best result. You can also use canned chicken if you like. Just make sure you rinse and dry it thoroughly before slicing it into thin strips. Poultry can be sliced thin or shredded, dabbed with a kitchen towel, and placed on a mesh dehydrator sheet. These are dried at around 145°F for 8 hours or more - or until everything is fully dried. Throughout the drying process, check if any fat has surfaced and blot with a kitchen towel.

Should you choose to dry ground meat, pick a chunk of lean meat and have it grounded at the butchers. Ground meat packed in stores and sold already ground in shops tends to be a bit fattier, so it is best to avoid that. It should also be cooked first. Fry up the meat with no oil until it is cooked through. Spread the cooked meat on top of a kitchen towel to allow most of the fat to be absorbed before spreading it on top of the dehydrator mesh sheet. The same is true with the chicken - it should be dried at 145°F for 8 hours or more, or until everything is fully dried. During the drying process, occasionally blot it with a kitchen towel to absorb the fat. After the process, the resulting meat should be crumbly and hard. It should also be colored darker than the freshly cooked ones.

Red meats and wild game share the same process when you plan to dehydrate them. For red meats, ask your butcher for the leaner parts and have them trim the fats off. On the other hand, wild game that is freshly caught should be properly dressed as soon as possible. Then check the meat for there is any sign of contamination - like fecal matter. Game meat shouldn't be dehydrated if it is contaminated. Choose the leaner cuts that are usually taken for roastings and cut away any visible fats.

For thinner strips of meat, boil them in the water or steam them until fully cooked. For bigger chunks of meat, bake them until they are fully cooked. Then cut it up into smaller cubes or strips. Remove any bone, gristle, and fat before letting kitchen towels absorb the excess fats and juice. Spread the meat on a dehydrating mesh evenly and dry at 145°F for 8 hours or more - or until everything is fully dried. Throughout the drying process, check if any fat has surfaced and blot with a kitchen towel. To check if they are dry, the meat should visibly look hard and dry and will be very difficult to cut with knives. If you can squeeze the meat and it bounces back, dry it again for a few hours more.

Jerky is basically dried thin slivers of meat - sometimes seasoned ground meat shaped into strips. But what gives them a category of their own is the seasoning that comes with it. Most jerky you see in stores are smoked and dried; others are cured and dried. It's the mixture of herbs and sauces that make it different from normal dried meat. It is also a lot chewier than the latter since most jerky marinades will include an acid as a tenderizer, i.e., vinegar or lemon juice.

These are combined with various spices and herbs that you can soak your meat in for an hour or more. A basic jerky marinade will contain soy sauce, Worcestershire sauce, pepper, and onion powder. Some even add liquid smoke. But for an authentic flavor, try smoking your meat first after marinating before processing them in a dehydrator. Another way is to fry the marinated meat in a skillet or bake it in an oven. Pat it dry with a kitchen towel to remove excess oil and spread on a dehydrator mesh. Set the temperature to 145°F and let it dry for 8 hours or more - or until everything is fully dried.

Throughout the drying process, check if any fat has surfaced and blot with a kitchen towel. Some jerky is not actually fully dried - this is done to retain the chewiness of the meat that is a benchmark for jerky; otherwise, it will be too tough to chew. Check in the drying jerky every

2 hours or so. A good jerky must not crack when bent, so adjust the timing as you see fit.

For those who have convection ovens, it is very easy to dehydrate food with them. Some ovens even have a special dehydration mode. But even if they don't, you can just set the temperature to 120°F to 140°F for fruits and vegetables, and 140°F to 160°F for meats. Place the food items spread out on drying racks or oven dehydrator trays. This is basically what a dehydrator is made of. These trays allow hot air to circulate across all surfaces of the food, making sure everything is evenly dried out. Arrange the food in a single flat plane with no overlaps. Set the appropriate temperature and set the timer to 6 hours or more, and let it run its course.

Storage

When done right, dehydrated foods can last for a few months to a year at room temperature. And most of the time, if you store it in the freezer or vacuum seal the food items immediately after dehydration, you can extend the shelf life even further. But even so, there will still be limitations on the shelf life of dried foods. No matter how well you follow the process and dehydrate them to the best of your ability, there will still be external factors that can affect its shelf life. For instance, dried food will still grow mold if you store it in a humid environment. Storing it under direct sunlight is also a no. Not only will sunlight shorten the shelf life, but it will also cause the nutrients to be lost.

Try to keep your dehydrated food items vacuum-sealed or placed in an airtight container. You can consider using canning jars, mylar bags, vacuum packing, and airtight mason jars. Store it in a cool and dry place and avoid sunlight and too much humidity. If you are using glass jars and vacuum packing for your storage options, you should consider adding desiccant packs in with the food items as an extra measure, especially if you plan on opening and closing the jars repeatedly. Desiccant packs remove moisture while oxygen absorbers take away oxygen. The latter is more suited for canning jars and mylar bags.

Meats will last approximately 2 months at room temperature and less when the meats have higher amounts of fat. However, 2 months can turn into 6 months if you keep them vacuum-sealed in the freezer. Fruits, on the other hand, can hold off spoilage for longer with their higher sugar content. You will find that fruits can be stored for a year or more, especially if you use vacuum packing.

Do's and Don'ts of Meat Preservation

My large Italian family is big on hygiene and safety, especially since we run a deli. Nonno is in charge of the meats, while Nonna is what we fondly call our "food safety officer." She would go in every morning and after hours to make sure everything is spotless, or we boys would get an earful from her. It goes without saying that Nonno is very careful with our products too. After years of experience running a multi-generational deli, we sat down around the dining table one night and proceeded to write down some of the do's and don'ts you should know about food preservation.

1. Trust your senses.

If something looks, tastes, or smells off, don't eat it. A wasted piece of meat is cheaper than a trip to the hospital—I can't stress this enough. Our ancestors got on living by trusting their senses, so you should too. If it looks like something is wrong and it smells wrong, don't hesitate to throw it out. Sometimes there are telltale signs, like molds and a weird color change; sometimes, there aren't. Even if it should be ok after 5 months, but at the 3-month mark, you see some spores growing, it is better not to risk it. I mean, do you honestly want to consume anything that looks like it might infect you with the zombie virus? No, thank you.

2. Use only fresh meat.

You should purchase your meats from a reputable source that you can trust. Butchered meat should be fresh, clean, and free from contamination before processing to lessen the risk of contamination. I suppose it goes without saying that anything that's fresh is always the best option, regardless of if it's meat or veggies. Fresh meat has a higher quality to it, tastes better, and can keep longer too.

3. Store your meats properly.

Speaking of keeping, storage is an art in itself. In the deli, we have a freezer room and humidity-controlled cabinets that cost a pretty penny. You don't have to buy those things, of course, since we're all about economizing for the home user here. Just store your items in an airtight container - vacuum-packed if you have a sealer - and store it in a cool, dry place. There's a reason why food packaging meant for shelf storage always has "store in a cool, dry place" written in big, bold letters. These big companies obviously don't want to get sued, right? So follow their well-meaning advice—this is not the time to be a daredevil in the kitchen. Take the adrenaline junkie inside you somewhere else because being adventurous when it comes to storage, expiration dates, and spoilage will land you an express ticket to the hospital.

4. Be aware of contamination.

The chances of getting it are really small, but it shouldn't be taken lightly either as this disease is fatal. C. Botulinum, the bacteria that causes the disease, is highly resistant to not only heat but chemicals too. It also thrives and grows in environments without oxygen when given the right temperatures - 78°F to 95°F. It is also reported to survive even at temperatures as low as 40°F to 120°F. That's why it is urged that people cook their meat, so the internal temperatures are at 140°F.

Another thing you should be careful about is mold. I know some of the best dry-cured hams from Italy are covered with mold, and they are one of the most delicious things in this world. But as long as you don't know what you are doing and you do not know what kind of mold has sprouted on the meat you're curing, then it's best to just chuck it. Cutting the mold out won't help either.

There are different colored molds. The ones you see in Italian hams are usually the white powdery kind that is a form of penicillin, an antibiotic, which is still widely used today. There are even spray-on mold cultures for sale to coat your dry curing meats with. These can effectively protect the meat from anything else contaminating it. However, some forms of white mold, like the furry ones, can be bad. Also, avoid all other colors of mold, from green and blue to deadly black.

5. And lastly, clean.

I must have written this again and again for every chapter of this book, but I'm going to repeat it again. Practice hygiene in your kitchen or workspace. Do not mix raw food with cooked food. Wash hands after handling anything. Use clean and sterilized equipment, utensils, and containers. Wipe down countertops all the time. Your workbench must be kept clean and tidy to avoid contamination because food safety is a serious business.

Here's the thing: you might think that a simple wipe down on your countertop is enough to keep your area clean, but when I say that you should tidy up your place, you need to make sure that everything is spic and span. I know that it can be extremely tempting to just leave everything as they are or to put off cleaning up after yourself until later, but the more you leave all that gunk lying around, the more they'll accumulate unwanted bacteria.

There's a reason why I'm adding this section and emphasizing cleanliness here—most meat curing newbies think that since they're doing all this from scratch and their homes are pretty clean, they can skip the sanitation part of the process. But sadly, tons and tons of consumers fall ill just because their cleanliness practices fell by the wayside a little bit. Even washing raw chicken is dangerous, as the running water splashing on the raw meat can splash droplets everywhere, from all around the sink to your clothes, hands, and even your face.

So, be absolutely sure that you can keep your workspace clean and sanitized—think of it this way: you're not only keeping yourself free from any harmful illnesses, but you'll also protect your family, friends, or guests in your home by saving them from an expensive trip to the hospital.

Conclusion

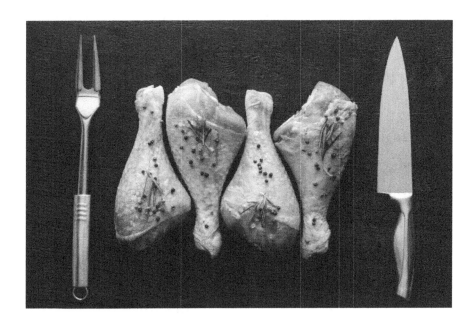

Whew! That certainly felt like a long journey, and I think we've pretty much covered everything from A to Z. Thank you for going through this adventure with us. Nonno is thrilled to have been able to impart knowledge to you. Throughout the writing of this book, we had experimented, researched, and ate a lot of our experiments - tasty or not, waste not want not. Some are fun - like the small batch of *chuno* we did. Some are successful - the jerky. Some are downright exasperating - like trying the infamous freeze-drying in the freezer until everything turned black. It was fun talking to Nonno and my father, picking their brains after dinner while drinking beer. This book has covered techniques that I would like to think are part of human history that you can still touch and taste in today's modern world. It would be sad to see it get lost.

Meat preservation is fun and shouldn't be scary or intimidating at all. If our ancestors can do it and figure it out through trial and error without any help from modern technology, then it should be easy for you too. So go on - enjoy your new hobby and don't hesitate to drop by our channel or in our stores. Share your newfound passion with us, and we'd be happy to help and guide you. It has been an adventure - writing this book has just increased my passion and appreciation for my work in the deli. It made us want to travel the world and see and taste what other cultures have come up with. Who knows? Maybe in our next book, we'll talk about how different cultures preserve their food! Ciao!

Made in the USA
Coppell, TX
17 February 2024

29123298R00085